ISBN: 978-1-4624-0124-6 (sc)
ISBN: 978-1-4624-0123-9 (e)

Library of Congress Control Number: 2012936996

Inspiring Voices books may be ordered through booksellers or by contacting:

Inspiring Voices
1663 Liberty Drive
Bloomington, IN 47403
www.inspiringvoices.com
1-(866) 697-5313

Because of the dynamic nature of the Internet, any web addresses or links contained in
this book may have changed since publication and may no longer be valid. The views
expressed in this work are solely those of the author and do not necessarily reflect the views
of the publisher, and the publisher hereby disclaims any responsibility for them.

Any people depicted in stock imagery provided by Thinkstock are models,
and such images are being used for illustrative purposes only.
Certain stock imagery © Thinkstock.

Printed in the United States of America

Inspiring Voices rev. date: 5/07/2012

Deception
Today's Church

God's Church or Satan's Army?

Simon Peters

Inspíring Voices®

A Service of **Guideposts**

Dedication

I am dedicating this book to the teachings of Francis Raleigh and all the Francis Raleighs throughout the family of God, whom I love in Christ. Also in response to God's calling in His three postcards to us, as taught by Francis Raleigh (2 John, 3 John, and Jude).

2 John (NAS)

God calls for us to watch ourselves and not lose what we have accomplished. God directs us to not allow anyone to go too far in their teaching of Christ. God, through John, directs us to maintain "exact scripture" teaching; allowing someone to blur the teaching makes us a participant in that evil.

3 John

Francis Raleigh very correctly teaches that evil has entered the church. Francis says it is our obligation to confront evil in the church and get it out.

Jude (NAS)

God calls us to defend and protect the Gospel. Through Jude, the brother of Jesus, God directs us to earnestly contend for the faith. We are informed certain persons have crept in unnoticed who practice "licentiousness"—that is, they have a disregard for strict rules of correctness. Francis Raleigh teaches we should not compromise the Word. We should not allow "blurring" of the Word. We should "fight the good fight." Because of "their own lust," being "worldly-minded" and "caring for themselves," we should save some by snatching them out of the fire.

When we contend for the faith that God has entrusted to us, we take a stand for Jesus. We will no longer compromise His Word or allow the truth of the Gospel to be misused or twisted. We will stand for Christ, and that will be enough for us.

God Is God

God deserves our worship and praise.

God deserves our undivided devotion—which is first place.

Illustrate the actions of today's church leaders.

Compare God's Church with today's church.

Address deception, in church, in life.

Give direction back to God, the Bible.

Awaken the lost.

People are the same, today and three thousand years ago.

God speaks to us.

NOTE: *All scripture references are from the New International Version (NIV) unless otherwise stipulated.*

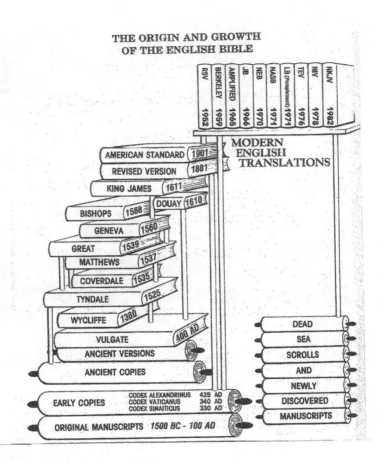

THE ORIGIN AND GROWTH
OF THE ENGLISH BIBLE

MODERN
ENGLISH
TRANSLATIONS

RSV	BERKELEY	AMPLIFIED	JB	NEB	NASB	LB (Paraphrased)	TEV	NIV	NKJV
1952	1959	1965	1966	1970	1971	1971	1976	1978	1982

AMERICAN STANDARD 1901
REVISED VERSION 1881
KING JAMES 1611
DOUAY 1610
BISHOPS 1568
GENEVA 1560
GREAT 1539
MATTHEWS 1537
COVERDALE 1535
TYNDALE 1525
WYCLIFFE 1380
VULGATE 400 AD
ANCIENT VERSIONS
ANCIENT COPIES

EARLY COPIES   CODEX ALEXANDRINUS 425 AD
                CODEX VATICANUS 340 AD
                CODEX SINAITICUS 330 AD

ORIGINAL MANUSCRIPTS 1500 BC - 100 AD

DEAD
SEA
SCROLLS
AND
NEWLY
DISCOVERED
MANUSCRIPTS

Chart courtesy of Back to the Bible broadcast

Why Me?

This book is the result of my starting to say yes to God's desires. It is our human nature, or it seems to be our nature, to typically say no to God. We justify saying no to God with excuses, such as, "It is not God; my conscience is playing tricks on me," "This is something I want or think should happen," or, "It is not really God moving me." We negate God's speaking to us with our excuses and lack of desire to respond to Him in a positive manner. We, as Christians, are spoken to by God continually, day in and day out. We often just ignore Him or are so involved with ourselves that we refuse to accept the fact that God is prompting us. God says in His Word that He does not come to us in the earthquake, violent storm, heavy rain, or any other catastrophe that appears. He speaks to us in a whisper. Therefore, the problem is not that we do not hear Him; it is that we are not listening for Him.

Since the beginning of time, God has wanted to establish a relationship with us. He created Adam and Eve, as well, to be in an intimate relationship with Him, and they were. He gave us all the freedom to choose. We have the right to choose to obey or to disobey, to be obedient to His will or to seek after our own. Unfortunately, seeking after our own will has continually been a problem for mankind, and God calls it wickedness. God's Word says we must die daily. This battle of choosing our will or God's is something we have to deal with 24/7. We must work on it consciously and constantly. I, just like you, had that same problem, habitually. I have, over the years, said, "No, it is not God; it is me." I have used every excuse, as many of you have, to say no to God. We do not

> **Exodus 4:13**
>
> But Moses said, "Pardon your servant, Lord. Please send someone else."

1

want to do the things God calls us to do, as simple as some are. We are so selfish and so into our wants that we ignore His.

I have ignored God's desires for many, many years. In fact, over six years ago, God called me to write a book. *Why should I write a book? Who am I to write a book?* I questioned myself, I questioned God, I made excuses, and I put it off and I put it off and I put it off. And, in fact, how many of us can say that we know God has wanted something from us, but we have put it off for such and such amount of time. I have put off writing this book for God for over six years, until God finally got my attention and brought me to the realization that saying "no" is not an option any longer—at least not a usable or workable option.

So, I am writing this book about the things I think God wants us to grasp. God wants a personal relationship with each of us. He has wanted that for thousands of years, and He is unchanging. God is perfect. He is God. There are those who say God changes His mind. God's word actually says, "He relents." If you are in tune to His Word, you know what He wants to do in His anger is to punish us, which is what we need and deserve. But He relents from His anger when we humble ourselves and pray. We will see that reflected throughout this book. The fact is that He says in His book, the Bible (*Basic Instruction Before Leaving Earth*), He has compassion and will relent and forgive if we will humble ourselves and pray and seek Him and turn from our wickedness. As well, if we do these four things in our lives, He will heal. We seem to ignore the fact that God wants a loving relationship with each of us. Our leadership in the church over the last seventeen or eighteen centuries has not made this truth a prerequisite in the

Hebrews 10:25 (KJV)

Not forsaking the assembling of ourselves together, as the manner of some is; but exhorting one another: and so much the more, as ye see the day approaching.

teaching. We, as pastors and teachers, are going to be held to a higher accountability. That is, we will be judged more strictly. Why would we ignore or attempt to ignore the precept God has established throughout His Word? The precept is that He, God, wants to be in communion with each of us and He wants us to desire that same loving relationship with Him. The first five books of the Bible, written by Moses and called the Pentateuch, illustrate most vividly this presence of God. The laws and directions given by God are to give us understanding and direction to Him. Even the sacrifices were to be given at a place designated by God where His people would gather to revere Him. God had Paul write in Hebrews 10:25 not to forsake the gathering of ourselves together as the manner of some is. However, many of us do not feel the need to gather together. We want to take the Word of God and make it say what we want. We want it to be our way. The Bible tells us that is exactly what is going to happen. Paul said that as soon as he walks out of the congregation, there are those in that congregation who will twist things around to make the message the way they want it. God had Paul also write that these same changers of the gospel message will gather around themselves a great number of teachers to say what their itching ears want to hear. There are many reasons we could apply to why we change the message, but the fact is we do. This liberalism has taken control of the church and it has been this way for centuries.

As you and I continue through this book, we will see the liberalization of the church. We will learn to recognize the deception we as preachers and teachers are involved in. The truth of the matter is, we lie. We believe we have good reasons for why we lie, but the fact remains—we lie. All lies come from the father of lies, Satan. We lie about anything we want. Again, we want the message our way. We lie about tithing. We

> **Luke 13:3**
>
> I tell you, no! But unless you repent, you too will all perish.

lie about drinking and gambling. We lie about sin. We lie about so many different things that we really do not know what is true and what is a lie. We will talk more about this subject later. Always remember, the truth is found within the parameters of God's Word, and it is our responsibility to know the truth.

We will be looking at many of the doctrinal failures of today's church. There will be issues that go 180 degrees away from society and our social teaching. I was taught when the ruling government under Constantine embraced Christianity as the religion of Rome, this was a grand and great thing. The church was no longer persecuted. The fact is, when we look at the last seventeen to eighteen hundred years from the perspective of God's Word, just the opposite is true. When the church embraced Rome, we became friends with Rome. That is, there was an alliance between Rome and the church. We look at this union from a world view and it looks great because people are no longer being thrown to the lions. However, throughout the Old and the New Testaments, God's Word condemns any kind of an alliance between God's people and the world. Soon after Rome embraced Christianity, the world went into one thousand years of the Dark Ages. The church has been struggling ever since the marriage of the world (or Rome) and the church. Does God confirm His message since the alliance of the world and the church? Did God confirm His message prior to the alliance? God had James, Jesus' brother, write that friendship with the world is hatred toward God. Therefore, the church has struggled for the last seventeen to eighteen hundred years to get away from the influence of the world because of this alliance. As we go through this

2 Peter 3:9

The Lord is not slow in keeping his promise, as some understand slowness. Instead he is patient with you, not wanting anyone to perish, but everyone to come to repentance.

book, there are going to be many things just as controversial, which will show the deception of man and the devil. We will be looking at my nearly thirty years of life in the church. As we view my experiences, hopefully you will recognize deceptions you never noticed before. The intent is to reveal, recognize, and make the changes necessary to our church, individually and collectively, to be within God's will, not man's. Maybe God will relent from His anger and again confirm His message, when it is His message.

I have had pastors say, "God only confirmed His word during the apostolic period." Yes, I cannot argue that it does seem to be a fact, but why? God is unchanging. Hebrews 13:8 says, "Jesus Christ is the same yesterday and today and forever." What has changed from the first-century church to the church of the last several centuries? If God is unchanging, the message must have changed for God not to confirm the message. The members of the first-century church were all in total devotion to God. Today's church is somewhere between total devotion and non-belief. We do not trust or obey. The problem is there is no in between. Jesus said, "He who is not with me is against me, and he who does not gather with me, scatters." Jesus is telling us there are no spectators in His church.

If you are not gathering (being a positive witness for Christ), you are scattering (being a poor example of what it means to be Christlike). To be a Christian, you must be active in the harvest of souls for God.

This book is being written because God has convinced me that telling Him no is not an option. I will describe my nearly thirty years in the church and what I had to experience before I said, "Yes, Lord." The

John 1:12

Yet to all who did receive him, to those who believed in his name, he gave the right to become children of God—

idea is that, hopefully, seeing my plight, you will not have to experience the same tribulations that I have had to go through for God to get a "yes, Lord" response. My prayer is that God has His will in this book and that His Holy Spirit is not only directing me but leading me in everything I write.

I hope the church sees that the world and the church do not mix. The church of today has many problems, all of which are of the world. There will be many subjects brought up that will, at the very least, cause debate. I hope and pray that with each one you will test the subject against God's Word. Many things you may not agree with when you first read them. Please test it against the Bible. I believe you will find that everything I am writing is factual. The truth is the truth. It hurts sometimes. Sometimes it is not something we want to be part of but we must. Our eternity depends on our obedience. We must put into practice the dictates of God.

Romans 8:23

Not only so, but we ourselves, who have the firstfruits of the Spirit, groan inwardly as we wait eagerly for our adoption to sonship, the redemption of our bodies.

A Note to My Family

Many of you can relate to this story about my family. I would like to take the opportunity to speak openly and honestly. Unfortunately, we do not always speak this way for fear of offending each other or just causing problems within the family. We as individuals do not want to be told anything. We think we know it all or that what we think is just as good as what anyone else thinks or believes. We believe our opinions are probably better than the next. It is something our father, William D., taught us—to think for ourselves. We loved him and liked him. We all like to do things our way, or my way, as Frank Sinatra and Elvis Presley sang about. It is a family trait that we are very good at, and it has worked well for us in dealing with the world. Yes, the family traits of thinking for ourselves, doing things *my way*, and being independent have worked well for us in dealing with people, getting along with people, and getting along well in our jobs. But unfortunately, doing it my way for eternal purposes will probably condemn us to hell. It is unfortunate that we do not know God's Word well enough as a family. Our beliefs are based on our opinions rather than seeking the truth from God's Word.

Dad was my best friend, my business partner, and my father. I loved him and still do beyond words. Dad was a great guy. Everybody liked Dad. He had a great heart. He was funny. People were drawn to him because he was open and forthright. He did not put on airs nor was he a respecter of persons. However, the chances of Dad being in heaven

> **Ephesians 1:5**
>
> he predestined us for adoption to sonship through Jesus Christ, in accordance with his pleasure and will—

are slightly above zero. God cannot nor will He allow anyone to spend eternity with Him in heaven who does not want to serve Him here on Earth. Each of us is responsible for our own salvation. Each one of us, brothers, sisters, cousins, aunts, uncles, mom … are all responsible for our own salvation. We need to know what the rules are. Why would we play the most important game of our life, which is where we will spend eternity, and not know the rules? We have to break the chains that have us bound. We have to know and honor God's desires. We are not to judge one another and we are not to pass judgment, but we are called to be fruit inspectors—we are to know God's children by their fruit. Where we spend eternity is completely in our hands. Why should we choose to think we are without rules? And even worse, why would we believe someone who tells us what the rules are? Read the Bible. Let's know what God really wants from us. It is so clear. It is so perfect. But we are actually clueless. We want to obey what we want, what we think, and not what we know.

I hear from each one in the family how you pray and so forth. The truth is, if you are not a child of God (within His will), He is not paying any attention to you. From cover to cover of the Bible, God is calling us into a relationship with Him. God wants us to recognize Him for who He is. We will never recognize Him if we do not know Him. We have to listen to God's words. If we want Him to hear our prayers, we must become children of the living God. We must turn from our selfishness, repent, be baptized, and receive the gift of the Holy Spirit. We must have the hope of adoption, through Jesus, into God's family. Read His Word cover to cover. Study it. Know it. We

Titus 3:6-7

whom he poured out on us generously through Jesus Christ our Savior, 7 so that, having been justified by his grace, we might become heirs having the hope of eternal life.

must not continue to deceive ourselves. Our eternity and the eternity of our children, grandchildren, and great-grandchildren depends on someone breaking the chains that bind us to our own deception. God decides who is to enter heaven and who is not. But God's decision is based on the result of our lives. God set the rules. He cannot, nor will He, change the parameters He has set. God is just. Jesus will judge by what he sees, to please Him who sent Him. When I look at our family over the last five generations, very few have any chance of being in heaven. Think about it: how many were born-again Christians? How many were baptized believers? How many loved God above all else in their lives? How many cared for God's family before themselves? These are the disciplines we must put into practice. Jesus paid the price for our salvation. Heaven is a free gift, but few will find it. Jesus said, "Children, how hard it is to enter the kingdom of God." It is hard to enter the kingdom of God because our selfish interest has us chained to the world and everything in it.

When we look at someone's life, the fruit should indicate "definitely in heaven." We want to relieve ourselves from concern so we want to believe that just about everyone is going to heaven. The truth is, most are not going to heaven. I hear people say, "They are in a better place now." If their lives do not indicate that they are in heaven by the visible fruit, they probably are not—and if they are not in heaven, they are not in a better place.

In Matthew 7, verses 13 and 14, God gives us a clear indication as to where we are as a people in relation to heaven. God tells us there are a lot of people on the road to the kingdom (or life). Unfortunately, most are on the broad road that leads to destruction. Only a few are on the narrow road that leads to life. The broad road is liberalism, wanting to

Matthew 24:35

Heaven and earth will pass away, but my words will never pass away.

get to heaven without putting into practice obedience. However, most people are not on any road. These are the people who do not attend church. We all need God's grace and His mercy. God does not want any of us to go to hell. But He leaves that choice up to us. We have no righteousness in and of ourselves. Our righteousness comes through the sacrifice of Jesus, and He alone is our righteousness. We can continue to do things our way, live life how we want. It's our choice. Life here on Earth is but one grain of sand on the beach of eternity. Why would we sacrifice eternity with God, which is like all the grains of sand on the beach of eternity, for one grain of selfishness? All God asks of us is that we get to know Him, understand Him, and serve Him by serving others. We should do this as an act of thanksgiving for what He has done for us through Jesus. God wants us to humble ourselves before Him, pray, seek Him, and turn from our selfishness. When we do, He will do miraculous things for us and through us.

We need to read God's word. We need to hear Him speak to us. We need to realize He is God, the creator of this universe and all that is in it. How completely unbelievable it is that this awesome, unimaginable, loving, compassionate, and just God wants to be close to you? He wants to be in a loving relationship with each of us. Why do we choose to ignore Him? God asks so very little from us. God wants us to turn from our selfishness, repent. He wants us to be baptized. He wants to take residence in our lives through His Holy Spirit. That is, die to self and be born again in Him. He wants His rightful place in our lives, which is first place. God wants us to share the Good News with others.

---

1 John 2:27

As for you, the anointing you received from him remains in you, and you do not need anyone to teach you. But as his anointing teaches you about all things and as that anointing is real, not counterfeit—just as it has taught you, remain in him.

Jesus said, "We must love the Lord our God with all our hearts and with all our souls and with all our minds. This is the first and greatest commandment." Then He also said, "Love your neighbor as yourself." James, Jesus' brother, calls this the royal law. Please pray, and then read God's Word. Get to know God. Hopefully you will grow to love Him the way He loves you, which is completely.

As you read this book, my prayer is that you will be driven to seek God. I pray you will seek to know Him and understand Him. I pray you will desire to build a relationship with Him. I want my entire family in heaven. I want my children, my grandchildren, my mother, my brother and his family, my sisters and their families, my cousins, my aunts and my uncles, as well as my two new great-grandsons, I want us all praising God in heaven. We must accept His gift here on Earth and live lives that say thank you, Lord.

The deception of this life is not worth eternity apart from God. We cannot allow our own deception nor can we allow anyone else to deceive us. God repeats Himself over and over throughout the Bible: do not be deceived. Do not allow the devil to deceive you and do not deceive yourself. Do not allow a brother or a mother or a father or a preacher or a teacher or anyone to deceive you. Test everything. Allow the Holy Spirit of God to teach you and lead you in all things.

Jonah 1:15

Then they took Jonah and threw him overboard, and the raging sea grew calm.

Send Someone Else

I have known for more than six years that God wanted me to write this book. I have said no again and again and again. I have given every excuse in the world why I should not write a book. "I do not want to. I am not qualified to write a book of this nature. I do not want to cause division in my congregation or any other part of the church. I am too lazy. I do not have time. God does not really want me to do this. This is me wanting to have it done." I've used other excuses, but you know where I am coming from. This habit of saying no is something we do. God touches our hearts, and we quench His desires with our excuses and pride. The fact is, we are disobedient. When we say no, we are not serving God but are serving ourselves. God wants this book written so we can see ourselves. Jesus' return is near. The time is short for us to make the necessary adjustments in our lives to serve God and not ourselves. Hopefully, while looking at my experiences, you will be able to see mistakes that I and those around me have and are making. I believe God's intent is for the reader to recognize the pitfalls and make the proper adjustments without wasting the time and effort.

Make no mistake about it: I know reading God's Word is more important than reading this book or any other book. I, myself, would rather read the Bible than anything. I do not want to read anything but the Bible. I know that if we are not open to God's will and we are not listening to the Holy Spirit's movement, we are better off reading

> **Hebrews 12:11**
>
> No discipline seems pleasant at the time, but painful. Later on, however, it produces a harvest of righteousness and peace for those who have been trained by it.

these books to prompt us to be in God's Word. The Holy Spirit that is in us is able to teach us all things. We need no one to teach us except God. The problem is, we habitually say no. We are so ingrained with ignoring God, saying no, that we will not let the Holy Spirit teach us. So we need each other for accountability—to keep the body of Christ in submission.

Many people believe that we are all children of God. This just is not so. We are all part of God's creation but not His children. We who believe in Jesus, God gives us the right to become His children. God wants each and every person on earth to become His child. God desires for no one to go to hell, but God is just. He has set parameters that must be met. God came to earth in the person of Jesus the Christ to pay a debt not any of us could pay and satisfy. God created a way for us to be with Him in heaven forever. God offers us salvation through Jesus for free, but we must accept the gift and say, "Thank you, Lord." We must put into practice two commands: love God above all else, and love your neighbor as yourself. To give us a better understanding of what this means, God had Paul write in Philippians 2:3, "Do nothing out of selfish ambition or vain conceit, but in humility consider others better than yourselves. Each of you should look not only to your own interests, but also to the interests of others."

The debt is paid! Now, how we live our lives in thanksgiving through Jesus, in obedience to God, equals heaven or hell. We get to choose. We cannot work our way into heaven. Heaven is a free gift. But we must accept the gift and live thankful lives in obedience.

Many people believe a variety of things. There are a lot of different thoughts on the subject of truth. But there is only one truth.

John 20:21

Again Jesus said, "Peace be with you! As the Father has sent me, I am sending you."

Everything else is a lie. Anything less than the whole truth and nothing but the truth is a lie. God has kept His Word pure for more than thirty-five hundred years. God's Word, the Bible, is where truth is found. The thought that we are all children of God or that we are all going to heaven is ridiculous. The thought that God would choose someone to be with Him for eternity who did not want to be with Him in this life on earth is a real fantasy. I think it is ironic that so many people believe they are going to be with God for eternity but do not want anything to do with Him in this life. If you will read God's Word, you will know it will not be that way. I hope and pray that as you read these many pages, the Holy Spirit will teach you as He desires. I pray you will recognize similarities between your experiences and mine. I pray you will make the adjustments in your life as the Holy Spirit leads you.

We have many opportunities to serve an unimaginable, awesome, loving, and just God. But serve Him we must. There is no other option. I do not consider hell an option. Our future depends on whether we serve Him or we do not. We must be ever mindful that God is sovereign. The Bible is our blueprint for life, the basic instruction before leaving earth. It makes no sense to me to believe we will spend eternity with God if we do not know the rules He has put before us. Nor can we be outside those same parameters. As I said before, God first told me to write a book describing my experiences in the church more than six years ago. I said, "No, not me." I have come to the realization in the last few years that when God wants something, the best thing we can do is say, "Yes, Lord," and try to be obedient. God does love us and He disciplines those He loves.

Isaiah 6:8

Then I heard the voice of the Lord saying, "Whom shall I send? And who will go for us?" And I said, "Here am I. Send me!"

In the next few pages, I am going to explain how God convinced me that writing this book was the right thing to do. In fact, I know now, after these many years of questioning, saying no, and not understanding why me, that it is it not because I am special. There is nothing special about me. God has asked me to do many other things—some I have done, some I have not. But I have always, nearly always, questioned, why does it have to be me? Finally, in the last few months, I have come to the realization it's because I will. I am not specially attuned to do His will. I am not specially attuned to write this book. God has probably asked many of you to do this very thing, but like me, you said no. When God wants something done, it will be done. If God wants a certain person to do a particular thing, that person will do it. God will eventually get your decision to line up with His will if He really wants you to be the one (as in Jonah's case). You may get swallowed by a great fish but you will decide to obey. I wanted to be obedient within my parameters, but God wants us to be obedient within His parameters. He finally got my attention, and His will became my will. The point is, I want to be obedient. We have to come to grips with the fact that God is the potter and we are the clay. He is the creator; we are the created. We should desire to be what God wants us to be, not what we want to be.

Matthew 7:7

"Ask and it will be given to you; seek and you will find; knock and the door will be opened to you.

Send Me

I have never been much of a risk-taker. I would usually assess the situation, decide what was right, or at least what was right in my thinking, and then go ahead. My mother, during my high school days, called me Grandpa because I was deliberate with everything I did. I started working for General Motors Corporation when I was eighteen years old, a few months out of high school. My father was a believer in saving money. Dad preached for us to pass up the little things, such as stopping at a fast food place every time you are out. This frugal thinking would allow us to make bigger purchases, such as cars and houses. Dad taught the entire family to think in this way.

As I said, I started working for General Motors at eighteen. My starting pay was $3.30 per hour. I immediately started saving $20.00 a week before I got my check. I did this by putting $20.00 a week into our credit union. This is something my dad did, so it seemed to me to be the right thing to do. I never stopped that habit. As the years went by, I increased the amount I saved each week. Over the years, that amount grew to many times the original $20.00. My goal was to retire from General Motors at the age of fifty-five years. I had a stretch goal of retiring at age fifty.

I bought, actually we built, my first house at the age of nineteen. I bought my first rental house at the age of twenty. My mother drew the plans for my first house. The house was very simple: three-bedrooms, one-bath, a kitchen, and a living room. My father showed me how to build a house and conserve spending. Actually, he did it. I just went

> **Ephesians 5:11**
> Have nothing to do with the fruitless deeds of darkness, but rather expose them.

along and paid the bills and learned. We subcontracted, that is we general contracted for ourselves, to build this first house. I kept the rental property until I was in my early thirties. I sold all of our rental property at this period in my life because it was taking so much of my time away from my wife and family. Rental property for people like me, who do not make large sums of money, is a great foundation for future financial growth. I built my second house at the age of twenty-eight. I designed and built this second house myself. Dad was always there, and it was a big help having a sacrificial brother who was a carpenter by trade. I worked six or seven days a week for General Motors as a millwright. I stayed busy. I stayed focused. I was quite successful with about everything I tried to accomplish financially. As I stated earlier, I am not a risk-taker; retiring with enough money to last the rest of my life was my goal at the age of eighteen.

As the years progressed, that continued to be my intent. Today, that is the talk of the financial world—to be financially sound before retirement. When I was forty years old, I designed and built my third home to live in. I was still working six or seven days a week at General Motors, and financially things just seemed to fall into place. I mean, everything was going just as I had planned and hoped for.

Most people would say I am blessed, and I would have to agree with them. I keep saying I did this, and I did that. The truth of the matter is, my wife worked outside the home all these years. She put up with my ambitions and our five children. I know I am the luckiest guy in the world. I believe that is true, but I realize I am the most blessed. I have been blessed by God for what He is allowing me to experience. But

> **2 John 10:11**
>
> If anyone comes to you and does not bring this teaching, do not take them into your house or welcome them.

the blessing of my life, my wife, Lucy, is unimaginable. As the years go by, I am in awe of her near perfection. She tolerates me, puts up with all my mistakes and problems, and continues to brag on me. I do not deserve her, but I thank God every day for her.

Things were going so well in 1995 that Lucy and I bought a two-bedroom, two-bath condo on the beach in Florida. We thoroughly loved that place. We loved being there. We normally went to Florida twice a year during the off-seasons. We would go down in May before the summer rush would start. We would also take a week or two vacation in September or October before the winter guest would come. We had a nice place and we loved it. We were right on the beach. Our intentions were to keep the condo and one day retire and spend our winters there.

We had built three houses for ourselves. Lucy and I liked the experience of building, although there were some ugly times along the way. We decided to start our own general contracting company and build custom homes in the latter days of our work life, before retirement. Our intent was to continue during our retirement. We did not want to be idle or unproductive. Essentially, our thinking was to build one or two homes a year. We did not desire to become large or to gain great wealth. We developed a corporation between Lucy and me. We decided to build a spec home as a means to establish the company name. We felt we had to sell our condo because we had a mortgage on our house and on the condo, and we were going to have a loan against the spec home. We did not want to risk the economy going south.

In 1999, we did sell the condo. We immediately built our first spec home. We were well pleased with our design, our location, and our

Colossians 3:9

Do not lie to each other, since you have taken off your old self with its practices price. The home sat on the market for ten months before it sold. The ten months the spec home sat waiting to be sold ate nearly every dime of profit in loan interest. We did not receive any contracts to build during the first spec home experience. Lucy and I were well pleased with the recognition we had received. We were extremely happy with the physical results of that first house.

We started planning our second spec home around Lucy's ideal home. I must say, her ideas were great. Lucy and I really liked the plans and felt good about starting this project. We bought the lot in the summer of 2001 and started construction on the first of September. We all know what happened on September 11, 2001.

We completed construction in May 2002. Unfortunately, I was diagnosed with asbestosis of the lungs on March 25, 2002. We put our home up for sale at the same time as the second spec home. Our home was more than $100,000 less expensive than the spec home. Our home sold first. So, we moved into the spec home. We loved the new home but it was really more than we wanted to have invested in living quarters and definitely more than we could afford. Because of my asbestosis, we dissolved the construction company and continued to try to sell the new house we were living in and enjoying. I give you all this information as background for what God was doing. Lucy and I had been growing closer to the Lord over the years. My daily prayer for myself was that I asked God for wisdom, knowledge, understanding, and discernment in everything. Sounds like Solomon, doesn't it? I prayed this as part of my daily prayer for twelve to fifteen years. I was fixated on not making mistakes. I hated making mistakes.

Deuteronomy 4:2

Do not add to what I command you and do not subtract from it, but keep the commands of the LORD your God that I give you.

Early in 2007, my focus had changed and my daily prayer had changed. I no longer was as concerned about mistakes as I was concerned about being what God wanted me to be. My daily prayer became, "Father, make me the son You want me to be." I knew then and I know now that where I spend eternity depends on whether or not I am the son He wants me to be in this life. I have to be His son in this life in obedience to Him in order to be His son in the next life—not by trying to work my way into heaven, but by saying thank you for the hope I have in Jesus in response to His sacrifice. My daily prayer remains, "Father, make me the son You want me to be." I make no bones about it. I want to be the son God wants me to be. I must say, God is faithful; if you ask, it will be given to you. If you seek Him, you will find Him. You have probably heard the cliché, "Be careful what you pray for." Sometimes the answered prayer is not exactly what you may have had in mind.

Sometime in early 2005, I was aware, or at least felt like, God wanted me to write a book describing my twenty-five years in the church. I was unwilling to do so. I used every excuse. I put it off. I said no. I argued with God about it. Thankfully, God is patient. As I told you, on March 25, 2002, I was diagnosed with asbestosis. My lungs looked like Swiss cheese with an additional half inch of plaque at the bottom of each lobe. At the time, I was sleeping on two or three pillows to elevate my upper torso. I would choke and cough and so forth during the night. I was having trouble sleeping. This is the reason I went to my family doctor, who sent me to a pulmonary doctor. The doctor said there was really nothing he could do for me except prescribe oxygen when I could no longer breathe on my own.

> **Proverbs 30:6 (NAS)**
>
> Do not add to His words Or He will reprove you, and you will be proved a liar.

Several months later, Lucy told me I should not be concerned with my asbestosis. She gave me a small laminated card with Acts 3:16 on it. Lucy told me at that time she was sure God had answered her prayers and given her this scripture as confirmation that I was healed. I sleep on one pillow now and have for the last several years. In December 2005, General Motors sent me back for chest X-rays, in adherence to OSHA regulations. The X-rays showed something but not like before. The doctor wrote on his report, dated December 15, 2005, "Review of previous computed topographic study indicates mobile bilateral pleural-based nodules, not apparent on this routine study of the chest." The doctor also wrote, "No obvious mass lesion, pneumonia, or congestive failure. The pleural-based nodules identified on a previous computed tomographic study are not apparent on this study."

God gave me the indication He wanted me to write a book; I balked at the idea. A few months later, I was sleeping more comfortably. I was sleeping on one pillow, not two or three. I no longer coughed and choked during the night. I got a medical report that recognized what was apparent before was no longer apparent. I still told God I was not the person to write a book for Him. I think there was something wrong with me. What do you think? To date, I still have no tangible evidence of ever having asbestosis. Thank you, God!

Lucy and I were still trying to sell an expensive house with large monthly payments. We had lost a lot of money during the 2000–01 time period. The situation with our investments did not look like it was going to improve anytime soon. We were invested in a variety of stocks with many different companies. In fact, nearly all our savings of over forty years was in stocks of various companies. My 401K through my work was fully invested as well. We held on to all these stocks until early 2007. I was disappointed with our investments and the fact we were still down over $200,000. So, in early 2007, I started selling everything, putting all our savings and *my entire* 401K into cash. Our savings was not as important to me but I did not want to lose any more money so I was moving everything into cash. Having money wisely invested for maximum return was no longer a priority. I was going to be sixty years old with over forty years with General Motors, so my intent was to retire in 2008. I was sure General Motors would have another buy-out of older employees in 2008. However, in October of 2007, General Motors stock fell to about $37.00 a share. Stock had been $43.00 a share in July 2007. I was accustomed to their stock falling in the fall season.

On October 19, 2007, I started buying huge chunks of General Motors stock. I felt comfortable doing that. In fact, I felt guilty because I was certain there would be a 2008 employee buy-out, which would make the stock rise again. I felt like I was involved in insider trading. Lucy got on me about buying so much General Motors stock. I can remember her saying, "This goes against everything you have taught all these years." The stock kept falling and I kept buying. It got so low that I was buying just to cost average. We all know what happened. General Motors went bankrupt. Lucy and I lost nearly everything in my 401K, which was over $200,000 when I started buying General Motors stock on October 19, 2007. We had over $300,000 in cash in our savings that I invested into General Motors stock. We lost all of that. Like Jonah, I had been swallowed by a large fish, a financial fish. And, like Jonah, I have decided to do what God has been trying to get me to do for over six years. Looking back, it is a shame that I so habitually said no.

We often believe we cannot do something or we do not have the right to do something or we do not have the expertise to do something. However, if God is for us, who or what could be against us? God can do anything. Nothing is impossible for God. We must be willing to accept His will and try to be obedient to it. For more than six years, I was not willing. I try not to let this lesson of arguing with God and being disrespectful to His desires be a distraction. I want this lesson to be nothing but positive. If I let myself dwell on the fact that I threw $600,000 and over forty years of work and savings away, it would and does hurt. But the truth is, I am more of the son God wants me to be now than I was four years ago. The savings, that attained goal, is no longer a distraction from God. I now use this experience to look at everything as an opportunity to serve Him. I try to make this experience foundational for never saying no to God. I would not be telling you the truth if I said it does not bother me. I miss buying whatever I want. I miss taking a couple of vacations a year. I miss feeling free to give money to my children and grandchildren, as well as anyone in need. But I realize that I have one less god in my life and that is a good thing.

Lucy and I were spoiled. We had money for whatever we wanted. We bought a new vehicle every year for each of us. We both worked and had good income. We felt secure financially. We traded our cars and paid cash for the difference. We had not had a car payment since 1987.

We almost went bankrupt ourselves after General Motors went bankrupt. We were so strapped for cash we had to borrow $25,000 against Lucy's vehicle to survive the first six months after General Motors' bankruptcy. My hours at work were cut. I was making about $3,000 less per month. We still had a large house payment. Things were very uncertain financially in 2008 and 2009. Lucy and I will be driving the same vehicles for years to come.

God had first place in our lives the same way He does in most Christians' lives. God was first but many things interfered with His allotted time. God was first, but children, grandchildren, ball games, plays, vacations, responsibilities, work, and many other things took time. We were cheating God. I was praying for God to make me the son He wanted me to be. Remember the royal law James talks about in James 2:8: "We must love God with all our heart, all our soul and all our mind, and love our neighbor as ourselves." More specifically, God says, "Consider others better than yourself." We can never expect God to work in and through our lives, as He desires to do, until we give Him his rightful place. God's place is first place or supremacy in everything. God is not to share first place with anything or anyone. He tells us He is a jealous God whose name is Jealous. If we allow our first place love to be shared, we may end up like Lot's wife.

God has persuaded me to do what I should have done six years ago. I will make public an account of my nearly thirty years of church life. I am sure most of you have similar experiences. In many of your experiences, you may not have recognized the situations for what they were. Looking at what I have gone through, you may be better equipped to recognize deception. I pray the world looking at my church experiences gives God the results He's looking for.

My Experiences in the Church

I attended a Baptist church with my mother and grandmother until I was about twelve years old. My mother stopped attending. I still went occasionally with my grandmother. Unfortunately, a few months after Mom stopped attending Sunday worship, so did I. I did not attend church during my teenage years, except on rare occasions. I tried to read the Bible three or four different times as a young adult. I just could not grasp anything from reading the scriptures. Lucy and her family never attended church, so when we married, church was not a priority in our lives. Early in 1984, we decided our children, ages eleven to seventeen years, needed a better foundation for life than she and I had given them thus far. We started attending a community church. After a few short months, the Holy Spirit was giving us fits. I should say He was giving me fits. I could not sit comfortably in the pew.

Finally, on November 18, 1984, Lucy and I accepted God's grace and mercy and were fully immersed into the baptismal waters. What a change since that time. I do not want to read anything except God's Word. God's Word is the only thing that makes sense to me. I must admit to the truth. I knew for twenty years prior to 1984 that God wanted something from me. I ignored His calling. I did not want to change my life. I did not want to be a religious nut. I kept saying no and ignored the prompting. But I knew God was knocking at the door of my life.

As often is the case, Lucy and I became very hungry for God's Word. We became very active in all areas of the church's activities. We were very active in the nursing home ministry. We became active in the homeless ministry as well. We had been serving about a year when I was asked to allow my name to be submitted for deacon. Many of us had conversations about me being a deacon before I said yes. I did not feel like I had been in the church long enough to be a deacon. I did not feel like I knew enough. I did not feel like I had a right. There were a lot of things the other deacons and the elders discussed with me before they convinced me to say yes and finally allow my name to be considered for deacon. I was elected deacon at the next election. The following year, I was elected chairman of the board of deacons and elders. I served as chairman, being elected every year for three years.

Lucy and I were driving twenty minutes to church each way four, five or six times a week. She and I had been discussing moving to another church closer to home. Lucy and I made the decision to make a move at the end of my term as deacon. I told our pastor I was not going to run for deacon again. He begged and pleaded with me to take another term because he needed me. There was some unrest in the congregation, but grumbling is commonplace, unfortunately. I agreed to stay and was elected deacon and chairman again. I believe it was four months after I was elected chairman that our pastor resigned and took another senior pastor position at a church in another state.

I spent the next several months hiring interim pastors, looking at applications, and interviewing to fill the preaching pastor's position. A few months later, we did hire a new pastor. The process of seeking a new leader of a congregation takes a lot of time, effort, and patience. There is a drain on each individual on the selection committee, on each member of the board of deacons and elders, and on the congregation.

Our new pastor was very different from our former pastor in a lot of ways. Our new pastor was older. He was much more assertive. He had more fire in the delivery of his message. He was Biblically confrontational. Our former pastor was not confrontational at all and very laid back. I used to tell him, "You are the only man I know who could spread crunchy peanut butter on a slice of bread and never see a nut." The difference in the two personalities soon came into play. Individuals who were not accustomed to being challenged took offense.

A few months later, I started receiving concerns from various members of the congregation. One morning, our morning service, which at that time was scheduled to end at noon and on occasion would run five or ten minutes over, ended at twelve thirty. The new pastor was on a roll; perhaps the Holy Spirit of God was in control. Later that afternoon, about three thirty, I received a phone call from one of the ladies in our congregation. She was extremely upset about the late dismissal. She was upset because her crockpot roast was ruined. I explained to her the pastor probably felt driven by the Holy Spirit to continue and that this is a rare occurrence. Running thirty minutes beyond our normal dismissal does not happen very often, if ever. She was not receptive to any explanation I tried to make. I reminded her of Acts 20 where Paul preached until midnight at Troas, and Eutychus fell asleep and fell from a third story window to his death. She immediately exclaimed, "That shows Paul preached too long." I did get to remind her that God was in the middle of that situation. God raised Eutychus back to life through Paul, placing his body over Eutychus' body. I do not believe twenty or twenty-five minutes cook time ever hurt anything in a crockpot. I think you get an idea of what I was dealing with.

The confrontational preaching, along with the difference in personalities of our former pastor and our current pastor, led to more grumbling than normal. After about a year and a half under our new pastor, Lucy and I decided to move on. I went to our pastor and told him we had decided to leave. I told him we had made this decision for our children as well as ourselves; we needed a change. I explained to him the grumbling, the shortage of help, and the lack of concern for God's desires throughout the congregation was a burden on our walk with God. Our pastor said he understood completely. He asked me if I would stay until the end of my term as chairman, which was just a few months away. He said he felt things would improve in a few months. He felt my departure would be less damaging then and he really needed my help. I naturally told him we would stay a few months and help in whatever way we could. Six weeks after my conversation with our pastor, he resigned. I was crushed. This was the second time in two years that a pastor had asked me to stay as a favor to him. In both cases, each was buying time for himself so he could make an easy exit (deception). All the other members of the board were aware of my concerns and our desires. Lucy and I had been completely open with our thoughts. I talked with the members of the board and explained that I felt gutted. I felt betrayed. I felt abused. I was amazed at what had happened—that two models of Christ could be so selfish and deceitful. I had believed in the integrity of both these men. I resigned as chairman of the board and deacon. I hated to give up, but I did not have anything left to give. I was truly crushed.

Lucy and I started visiting churches close to our home. I must admit there were several visits Lucy and the kids made without me. I was not bitter, but I was empty, void of feeling. I had believed in the sincerity of both our pastors. I really do not know how to describe where I was. I still had faith in Jesus but I was not ready to trust any man. Coming from a small congregation, Lucy and I agreed we did not want to attend the largest church in the area, which was Kingsland Community Church. Kingsland ran about eleven to twelve hundred people each Sunday morning. We visited several churches, some of them a second time. There was one church we visited three times. I do not know exactly what we were looking for … maybe nothing in particular, but we were both praying God would grant us a church home. We wanted to be where we could grow and strengthen our relationship with our creator and savior.

Our children wanted to visit Kingsland Community Church. Many of their friends went there. Lucy and I finally gave in. We did not think we wanted to be part of a church with that many people, but we visited and the preaching was from the Bible. The people were friendly and pleasant and we knew several members of the congregation. Most of us lived in the same community, and our children attended the same schools and participated in the same after-school activities. The service was thought-provoking, God-centered, worshipful, and praising. So, we attended again and again and again. Our children liked it at Kingsland Community Church, and so did Lucy and I. After about three months of visiting, we transferred membership. Lucy and I joined a small group for Bible study. We were again growing in our relationship with the Lord. It felt great to be back interacting with members of the body of Christ. Having God as our supreme priority in our lives is everything. We were running about eleven to twelve hundred in attendance every Sunday in two services.

Our leadership decided we needed to enlarge our worship center. The leadership hired a group from Texas to give us an idea of how much we could expect to get in a major building campaign. The group from Texas also provided the step-by-step strategy for securing these funds. My dictionary describes *strategy* as follows:

- The science of planning

- A plan based on this

- Skill in managing or planning, especially by stratagem

I think my concern was and is, if we were going to do something God wanted done, why pay a consulting firm $50,000 for their strategy? If it is God's will, who could be against it?

My vocabulary being limited, I had to look up *stratagem*. I again referred to my dictionary, and *stratagem* was described this way:

- An artifice, plan or scheme for deceiving an enemy in war

- Any artifice, trick or deception

These synonyms were listed for *stratagem*: artifice, ruse, blind, trick, subterfuge, chicanery, plot, snare.

I have a real problem with people preaching faith while leaning on the world as an example of faith. The group from Texas looked at our membership financially and a decision was made that we could expect to gather $5 million. We built a new sanctuary capable of seating over one thousand people. We also made a few other small changes, but the bulk of the money went for the new sanctuary and the mechanics it takes to support a facility of that size. We turned the old sanctuary into a gymnasium for the school. At that time, we offered a Christian school for children in grades one through five. The entire project went well, and the $5 million was rather easy to gather. The people from Texas really knew their stuff. The money, the building, the entire project was completed in less than three years. About a year after the construction project was finished, our leadership brought back the group from Texas. I suppose we were looking for another strategy.

The group from Texas was very capable. They came up with another strategy for us. We were going to start another building campaign. Raising $5 million in three years was awesomely astounding. Our senior pastor called it godly. This time we were to have a building project and renovation costing $12 million. The leadership told us that the growth projection for Kingsland Community Church was such that it was a must we do this $12 million renovation.

A few months later, the engineering firm had completed the building plans and they were made public. The sanctuary we had just built, capable of seating more than one thousand people, was not to change. We were adding many rooms, changing the location of our gymnasium, and changing the location of the cafeteria for the school. We were not changing the sanctuary/congregational assembly room at all. Many congregants started questioning the need based on projected growth. Many of our body started to complain that this was a $12 million project for the school. The grumbling was so bad and got so intense that Sunday after Sunday, our senior pastor stated from the pulpit that this expansion had absolutely nothing to do with the school—emphatically, with a show of anger.

Kingsland Community Church teaches from the Bible. The only discouragement I ever had with our teaching was our senior pastor, who was a PK. PK is what he called himself and other preacher's kids. Because he was a preacher's kid and felt like his parents spent too much time with the needs of others, he taught that pastors should spend a great deal of time with their children above and beyond the needs of the church body. I always felt like that teaching was a personal problem he had and was not consistent with God's word. God loved Jesus before the creation of the world. I am glad God did not think like James Cantrel, because God gave Jesus up as a sacrifice for you and me.

We had a congregational meeting one Sunday after morning services. The projected growth theme and the emphatic denial the project had anything to do with the school was maintained. We lost several members because of this project. Actually, it was not because of the project as much as the way it was presented. We lost one couple out of our home study group. They are friends with my wife and me, as well as our brother and sister in Christ. Chad and Mary's position was if they stayed at Kingsland Community Church, they would be accepting the staff and leadership's explanation of the project. That would make them just as guilty as the staff and eldership. God's word places Chad and Mary right on but I'm not sure about their leaving.

A couple of weeks after that first congregational meeting on the $12 million renovation project, our staff passed out a single sheet of paper with twelve areas where we as Christians should be committed. Each of the twelve examples was a Bible verse. Each verse was followed by the translation it was taken from, such as KJ for King James, NIV for New International Version, and so forth. One of the verses did not have the translation from which it came. That one was the only one that gave us direction for giving money. That is a red flag in about anyone's book. Young elementary school children would recognize the inconsistency. I checked every version of the Bible I had at home. I checked the King James, the New International Version, the Living Bible, the Good News, and the New American Standard. None were even close to the Biblical verse given as our direction for giving financially.

Being me, Simon Peters, I stewed over this for several days and then finally came to a point where I called the senior pastor. Pastor James Cantrell was not available when I called. I was asked if someone other than James could help me and I said no. James Cantrell ran the show at Kingsland, and I had thought about this long enough. I needed an answer from him so I left a message. James returned my call a short time later. We discussed the twelve Bible verses we were to live by and their point of origin. We particularly discussed the one that did not indicate its point of origin. James said he did not have anything to do with that handout. James said his associate pastor, Francis Raleigh, put that together. I must admit, I found it hard to believe anything that happened at Kingsland was not overseen and approved by James. But while I had James on the phone, I questioned him about the need, as stated, for a $12 million expansion that made no change to the size of our worship center or sanctuary. I was especially concerned about the continual claim that the project had nothing to do with the school. We discussed the issue for two or three minutes, and I was not accepting any of the explanations James was giving me. They did not make sense. In fact, it seemed like God was giving me the questions to ask him. Finally, James said, "Pete, what happens is the Sunday school classes will put things on the chalkboards and then the elementary school classes will come in on Monday and erase them. The elementary school teachers will put things on the chalk boards, and the Sunday school teachers will come in on Sunday and erase them."

I immediately responded, "How can you say from the pulpit over and over and over again, 'This $12 million expansion has nothing to do with the school?' What you have just told me means it has everything to do with the school."

James was obviously caught off-guard. Actually, he seemed shocked that he had allowed himself to be in that verbal bind. It took him some time before he responded. When he did respond, he said, "I think the end justifies the means." This made me speechless. I could not believe he actually said that to me. But he did.

I should mention that when Lucy and I were baptized into the family of God in 1984, there was a change in my personality. I was born and raised in a family where men gave firm handshakes and men did not hug or say, "I love you," as common practice. Men said, "I love you," by the way they lived. Men never openly showed a weakness, especially emotionally. Some time after baptism, I noticed I felt the pain of others. I was emotionally geared. I shed tears when others shed tears. I would emotionally tear anytime I thought of what Jesus had done for me. I was this way for ten or eleven years. I would cry watching movies because I related emotionally to the other person's situation. I felt what they felt. In all honesty, I did not mind it, although it was embarrassing sometimes, especially when my kids made fun of me. I liked being able to relate to others.

After my experience with James Cantrell justifying lying to his brothers and sisters, I lost that emotional tie to others. I guess I had become hard of heart. I believe at that time I was just going through the motions. I realized men were men. Unfortunately, just because someone is a pastor, he is not necessarily godly or even honest. Sadly, I know men and women who have left the church and have not returned because of the way this $12 million expansion happened.

After that, I went probably three years with the head knowledge of God, but I did not have the broken heart I once had. I told my wife I hated the fact that I had lost the awareness of others. I had lost the ability to feel what others felt, to immediately place myself in their painful situation and experience their brokenness. At one time, because of this emotional tie to others, I was embarrassed, but now that it was gone, I felt empty inside. I was especially concerned because what Jesus had done for me was just a reality. I was not emotionally broken when I thought about it. I told Lucy, "If God ever gives me that emotional awareness back, I will never allow someone else's evil to rob me of it again." Fortunately, as I said, this dark period only lasted about three years. God has again answered my prayers and granted me that connection to others. I am again emotionally charged. Thank you, Lord. I highly recommend allowing God to enter into your life in such a way that you give Him the freedom to move you emotionally. Allowing emotion to shine in my life is something I consider a privilege, and I feel God-honored. I feel more masculine now than I did when I controlled my emotions. I now allow anything to get to me. I suppose we are so selfish we really do not care, except for ourselves and our families. I believe this is the difference between a hard heart and a tender heart—someone led by the Holy Spirit and someone not led by the Holy Spirit. I remember that Jesus wept.

We attended Kingsland Community Church for a few more months after my conversation with James Cantrell. I must admit, my growth was on hold. In fact, as I have said earlier, I had become insensitive or hard of heart. Again, what troubled me most was the loss of emotion concerning what Jesus had done for me, taking my punishment. Now it was head knowledge and I was not brokenhearted. I just did not feel the pain, and that bothered me. I can legitimately understand why so many fall away from the faith because of the poor witnesses for Jesus, especially those who preach and teach.

Shortly after my conversation with James Cantrell, I believe four months, our associate pastor, Francis Raleigh, became senior pastor of the Chapel of the Flock Christian Church. Within six months after Francis left Kingsland, Lucy and I started attending Chapel of the Flock Christian Church. Lucy and I were at Kingsland Community Church about eight years. We have been at Chapel of the Flock Christian Church more than ten years.

The people at Kingsland Community Church were and are wonderful. The fact is, our youngest son is still at Kingsland and is very active there. He is a worship leader and Sunday school teacher. He works with the youth groups and senior high teenagers and spends a lot of time counseling. The people at Chapel of the Flock Christian Church are wonderful as well. We love our brothers and sisters at both places.

We had been at Chapel of the Flock Christian Church about two years when our leadership brought in the professional strategists from Texas. We had many people at Chapel of the Flock Christian Church who had transferred membership from Kingsland Community Church. Dozens of people left Chapel of the Flock Christian Church as soon as our leaders announced we were going to have a $5 million building fund campaign. Unlike Kingsland, where we as a body voted for the projects, however manipulated by the leadership's word game, at Chapel of the Flock, the leadership dictated what was going to happen. We borrowed $5 million. We built a gymnasium. We added some office space and renovated the old office area. We built a grand entry area or vestibule. The sanctuary or worship center remains the same. I asked our chairman of the Board of Elders, "Why are we doing this? Why are we spending $5 million and not doing anything to our worship center?"

His reply was, "That is what everyone else is doing, building gymnasiums."

I am not sure if the building success at Kingsland was too much of a temptation for Francis Raleigh or what. I really do not know. The truth is six or seven years later, we have a $15,000/month interest payment on a $5 million loan. We have a gymnasium that is almost never used, at least by the church body. The staff does have a nice set of offices. They have a nice place to come if they ever decide to do so. The best thing to come out of this entire building campaign for the membership, the people who are paying for it, is the fact the vestibule or entry area has become a place for people to converse before and between services. The vestibule has been a good thing. In my opinion, it is the only good thing for $5 million. It is one $125,000 - $150,000 room out of $5 million dollar expenditure.

After making the decision to saddle the congregation with a $5 million dollar mortgage, the leadership at Chapel of the Flock Christian Church decided the membership, the body of believers in Jesus, was not living up to our responsibilities. They enacted a new rule. Before anyone could become a member of this church, they must first take a class called Participating Members class. This explained what you as a member of the church must do. Upon completion, you must sign a written agreement that you will abide by Chapel of the Flock Christian Church's doctrine, including giving of your time and your money. This rule, or law change, was never announced to the membership. How it became apparent was when we as a membership started noticing that as individuals came forward during invitation, moved by the Holy Spirit of God, nothing happened, nothing at all. People were not being baptized. People were not transferring membership to our body of believers. They were being put off. They were being told they had to take this class.

Members started asking questions. We first asked among ourselves. I did not have any answers. I did not know what was going on. The staff would simply talk to these individuals when they came forward, and we as membership saw nothing else. As more and more members of the body were recognizing what seemed like a problem, discussions became more intense. We discovered our staff was telling these individuals moved by God that they had to take this class that we knew nothing about. Our leadership had changed God's plan for salvation. Enough of the members of the church body recognized the deviation from God's plan that there was pressure applied both verbally and in writing to effectively constitute another law change. Now a person can be baptized into Christ if they insist. They can therefore become members of God's church, but to be a member of Chapel of the Flock Christian Church, they have to take this special class and sign an agreement to abide by our doctrine and give of their time and money.

I realize at first glance this seems unusual. This points to the fact that the Church of the Living God and Chapel of the Flock Christian Church are two different churches. I always thought there was one church, one bride, meeting at different locations. I always thought there was just one body with many parts. I will let our pastors explain that to you shortly. It was explained to me this way: "It is our policy to police membership and more important, the responsibility of membership. Most churches across the United States are using some form of this participating members rule. This is to guide their members within that church's doctrine or teaching." So I was told by a pastor.

I said I would let our pastors explain their thought process with regard to salvation, membership responsibility, giving, and adding to and subtracting from God's Word. You may recognize their revelation of God's shortcomings and how they have been able to save the day from His oversight. The following is a word-for-word e-mail exchange between one lady in our congregation and three of our pastors who felt led to respond to her concerns. The e-mail starts:

Brothers in Christ,

I hate to write but I feel I must. Yesterday in first service when the mother and daughter (both Christians) came forward to place their membership with our local body at Chapel of the Flock Christian Church, they were denied until they completed a class we created. I was surprised, embarrassed, sad and distressed when I witnessed this statement and response to their commitment. We "put them off" for a later date. I have not read anything in scripture to justify this practice. Please ... if you have, tell me where. My heart sank both for them and the many others in the congregation who perhaps have been contemplating making a decision but for whatever reason have not yet done so. Specifically, a young man sitting in front of me who I have been praying would take that step of faith.

This morning as I was driving to work I was remembering back to the day I asked Christ to come into my life and take over (at age 30). I believe that had I been put off or asked to take a class first, it would have crushed me and might possibly deter me from taking that step. I felt inferior anyway since I had only recently been attending church and did not know the scriptures, stories, etc. The message this brought to me was that we truly cannot "come as we are" and allow God to change us ... we must first "do" some things for "man" and then be "qualified" to ask forgiveness.

In recent months I have truly felt that God was working in the body of believers at Chapel of the Flock (in leadership and the congregation) in a mighty way. I am sure that we are on the verge of something good that God is going to do in and through us and expect a revival of His church at Chapel of the Flock. What I am wondering after yesterday is … did we allow a kink in our armor and Satan jumped in? We must be so careful to be faithful to HIS WORD and not man's rules. I look forward to hearing from any and all of you as we continue to serve God together and bring people to Him (just as they are).

Serving Christ with You,

Lois

Response to the lady from one of our pastors:

Lois:

Thanks for writing and voicing your concern as you saw it. In answer to your questions; first membership is not a scriptural concept. Other than scripture referring to being members of one body of Christ there is no other directive in scripture that guides churches in how they pursue membership in their local body. And, I agree with you, we would not want to hinder anyone who wants to respond in some way. Our decision to tweak our membership requirements were so that we could have a place to communicate what is expected of members as they seek to join our church. Membership should be synonymous with following Christ. Under the old way of membership, if they were believers we shook their hand and they were "in" as members, possibly not having an appropriate conversation with a leader to understand what membership or following Christ really means. The "down front" experience with decisions on Sunday morning is often not adequate for what the person needs. We do the best we can on the spot but I find the people that come forward need more than what we can give them at the moment. As leaders, I think it is responsible on our part to make good disciples. The process includes an introduction to who we are and what we do, then giving people the opportunity to decide whether or not they want to join.

If someone comes forward responding to God for salvation or prayers, our process has not changed. We respond to that appropriately by either setting a time to talk further or taking their confession then and immersing. In this sense, we are separating the conversion of a person who becomes a member of God's church worldwide. But, then asking them to take the Participating Members class to understand more specifically how we follow God's unique call in this place and leaving it up to them whether or not to join. Understanding expectations are a powerful motivator. Jesus called those who followed Him to count the cost. And, our goal with the membership process is to provide a forum where we (God's leaders) can communicate some of those expectations.

I hope that helps. Please write or call me if you have further questions or want to dialog about this.

Blessings,

David Scott

And then another pastor responds:

I hear and understand your concerns. We have had the same discussion here in staff meetings as well. I see that David has also responded to you already but I'll toss my hat into the mix as well on this concern with hope that it does not cause confusion.

Our stance for becoming a Christian has not changed. Christ said we may come as we are to accept salvation and I for one am very glad that He made that the case. It is not our desire to communicate that salvation comes through our man-made membership class. Though since some associate membership and salvation as one thing, I can see how that can be confusing. Also, from your concern, it seems that we need to do a better job in communicating where we are coming from on this issue.

Our membership class is designed to assist with a culture issue we have observed. The day of being committed to a congregation and serving there for a number of years seem to be passing by us. More and more persons in our mobile society are moving frequently between different congregations for various reasons, and as a result are becoming less grounded doctrinally as well as spiritually. People who have moved between congregations which are not of our denomination are sometimes unaware of the Christian doctrines and expectations here at Chapel of the Flock. For example, it is not uncommon as the Children's Pastor for me to be asked about infant baptism for the salvation of someone's newborn.

In order to better educate people about what we believe and teach here at Chapel of the Flock, we developed the membership class. It is our hope that during the class people can learn our doctrinal stance, what we expect from members, and answer questions that arise due to the different church backgrounds that many people have.

Thank you though for bringing up this issue to us. I expect we'll address it again in staff meetings to come in order to determine how to better communicate our desires in educating persons becoming a Christian and also joining Chapel of the Flock Christian Church.

Mike Eaton

Then the senior pastor e-mails:

Lois,

Great observation! It is an awkward thing for the people who watch this take place who have worked their way toward the Lord, like you did, and then to need to attend a membership class seems to "slow the flow" for them. Membership is a needed relationship in the body of Christ. Paul formed local congregations and encouraged people to be active in living out their faith in that body and their community. We do the same but in recent years have found that without good instruction and teaching about what God expects of them (counting the cost) then we have many who become consumers rather than participants in the body of believers. I know to those of us who have been around Christianity for a while this seems awkward but as we are seeking to "make disciples" who will be responsible to the Word and their Lord.

Hope this helps some, Francis

Then the lady responds back:

Francis, Mike and David,

Thank you all so much for responding to my e-mail. I truly appreciate the fact that we can freely communicate. I was so glad to hear that we are not keeping anyone from giving their life to God in repentance and acceptance of His free gift of salvation. However, your comments did bring another question to my mind. Do we at Chapel of the Flock require (for membership in our local church body) people take the participating members class and signing the form in the back of the class book?

Lois

Response back to her:

Lois,

We do ask that they sign the form in the back to understand their response to the proposition of membership, baptism, or another issue they need to discuss. It is a means to appropriately follow-up with them. Often times it gives them the occasion to ask for time with a pastor to talk further about an issue they're dealing with.

David

I ditto David's response and agree that the forms help us to follow-up with people on specific issues or needs they have, especially if that is more teaching, etc. Thanks for being observant and concerned.

In Him,

Francis

October 10, 2007

Dear Pastors and Elders:

I've provided this trail of messages below just to keep everything together (they start at the bottom of the document).

I appreciate your truthful and open comments in reply to my questions. I understand, I think, the "why" of your policy but have some serious concerns that I would like to bring to your attention.

1. *It appears to be easier to get your name in God's "book of life" than the membership roll of Chapel of the Flock Christian Church.*

    - *God's grace is open to all who will repent and receive Jesus as their savior. We then live in free will grace with only one covenant— with God. If we truly seek God and continue to walk in Him, we'll certainly serve one another as we grow in our faith.*

    - *I don't believe it's scriptural to add to the requirements God put before us to be "born again" in our faith and serve with other believers.*

    - *I believe this sends a message that says, in effect, you can join God's family but … if you want to join 'our family at CFCC' you must first attend this class and sign this paper commitment. How does that extend God's grace and love?*

    - *Chapel of the Flock appears to be an elite club of believers that require works to enter. I do not believe this was the intent but*

I see it as the outcome. I also believe it sends a message to those contemplating accepting Christ and joining our group of believers, and not a good one.

2. *I've recently become aware of a single mother who is a baptized believer. She had been attending Chapel of the Flock and expressed interest in becoming a member. She was told she must take the Participating Members class first. Since she was unable to attend the class because of the practical life of a single mother, she moved on. What a sad shame ... instead of loving and encouraging her in our "body" we turned her away.*

3. *I am in full agreement with helping to disciple those in your flock and admire you for doing so. I wish I had that kind of training as a young Christian. In the midst of this good work, however, I believe something went amiss and we got way of track.*

I am and will continue to pray for all of us as we live and walk out our faith together in Christ. Thank you for listening.

In Christ's love,

Lois

I wrote the elders and the staff on this issue, as did many others. I chose this lady's trail of messages because I think our leadership did a wonderful job of explaining God's "not adequate" lack of directive in pursuing membership and the need to have members under signed contract. The pastors also pointed to the fact that people move from congregation to congregation for various reasons. God placed a void in every person. People try to fill that void with different things: drugs, sex, money, prestige, praise, honor, or power. There is only one thing that will fill the void, complete the puzzle, or satisfy the need, and that is God's presence. When people do not find God (truth) in one place, they will look further.

I do not know if you have formed an opinion of our leadership or not. I hope not. I would like to tell you more about them. First of all,

I want to tell you that they are good men. I like all of them, just as I like every pastor I have ever had. I have never had a pastor I did not like. Our senior pastor is married and has two children. His wife works as a receptionist for the church. Both of his children are adults. Our associate pastor, David, is married and has two teenage daughters. His wife is a school teacher. Our worship leader, pastor of communication arts, is married and has three children. His wife is a school teacher as well. We have six other ministers on staff, but I am not going to define each one. The fact is, each of our staff members are good men, good husbands, and good fathers. They are the kind of individuals you might choose as friends. This is true of every single pastor I have had in nearly thirty years. But are they Christlike? Are they role models, bringing a smile to God's face?

Probably because of the teacher influence, we shut our church down between Christmas and New Year's Day, except for Sunday. We also close the church at noon on Fridays. We celebrate all the holidays along with the school system by closing our office. We also give our pastors a three-month sabbatical over and above their vacations every five years or so. We at Chapel of the Flock Christian Church only have one service day a week. That is, we meet on Sundays only. We have three time slots on Sundays for Sunday school. The last two time slots are for worship service or Sunday school. We do have one other service on Wednesday night. But I will need to explain that service.

As I said, we only have Sunday services at Chapel of the Flock Christian Church. The small group my wife and I meet with on Tuesday nights recognized the need for a prayer service. One of the couples in our group was committed to the food pantry ministry for nine years. Over seven years ago, we started discussing the spiritual need of the individuals coming for food. The couple involved with that ministry told us there was never anyone there representing the staff or leadership of the church. This couple quit serving with the food pantry a little over a year ago. They had served in that ministry for over nine years. They never saw an elder or pastor at the food pantry, not for support, help, or prayer, in all those years. We as a group discussed this spiritual need at some length over a long period of time. We tried to come up with a solution. We talked about the need, the opportunities, whose responsibility it was, and what possibly could be done in talking with the staff and elders. No one wanted to take ownership of a prayer service. I hate to admit it, but we talked about it for over three years but never came up with a solution. Finally we came to the realization that no one was going to do anything. So, four years ago, my wife and I and another lady started a Wednesday night prayer service at Chapel of the Flock Christian Church. The thought at the time was that we would start this service and eventually one of the staff would take it over. We began in August 2007. Unfortunately, I am still facilitating it. Our thought that one of the staff would take it over was foolishness on our part. You cannot embarrass someone who enjoys idle time into going to work.

Starting in January 2010, our senior pastor started having the fourth Wednesday of every month's prayer service in the worship center and he facilitates that service. That is a good sign, a positive happening. Pastor Francis was led to at least take responsibility for that service. He was hoping, I am sure, to get more of the church involved. At the first fourth Wednesday night service, about one hundred and seventy-five congregants attended. The numbers quickly fell off. After about six months, the numbers fell below fifty and unfortunately, by the fall of 2010, the numbers were below thirty-five. The numbers for the Wednesday night service facilitated by Francis Raleigh for 2011 are running about twenty-five people each fourth Wednesday. Sadly, the other Wednesday night prayer services that I facilitate in another part of the building run six to twelve in attendance. The first two years during the winter, there were Wednesday nights where Lucy and I were the only two in attendance. Our Sunday attendance is about twelve hundred people. The last three years, two years solidly, there has been another couple who is sacrificial in their commitment to meet with the Lord and pray for the needs of our congregation, individually and collectively. I would like to say my heart goes out to the three or four individuals who put into practice what God asks: to serve. They know they are not perfect in and of themselves, but they are willing to give of their time to do the one thing we can do for others and that is pray for one another.

I have spoken to Francis Raleigh about the poor attendance on Wednesdays. He told me that he, cannot get his staff to attend prayer services. I told him in truth it is his fault. Francis teaches the same message as James Cantrell. God must have first place in our lives but our spouse and children and our parents (family) come before all others. I told him I do not believe this is consistent with God's Word, and this teaching is a foundation for apathy in the congregation, elders, and staff. As I said before, I am glad God did not think like these educated men. We would all be going to hell for eternity.

Some facts about the Wednesday night prayer meeting I have facilitated for the last *four years*:

- Only one elder has attended, one night only.

- One pastor came twice, three years ago.

- Francis Raleigh has attended six or seven separate times over four years.

- On the fourth Wednesday of the month, usually one pastor and one elder will show up. We have twelve elders and nine ministers.

- Sometimes Francis Raleigh is the only member of leadership in attendance on the fourth Wednesday.

Pastors and elders are role models. Our Wednesday night prayer meeting is a perfect example. Pastors and their families put a very low value on meeting with God to pray. The watching congregation has the same value system. I personally would rather be a Major League ballplayer on steroids than a pastor who ignores his flock and God. Unfortunately, Chapel of the Flock Christian Church is not in an unusual situation.

Most, not all, but most pastors are so caught up in the world, God is but an avenue for easy income.

Our congregation, of course, is a mirror image of its leaders. The acorn does not fall far from the tree. We know and recognize that the churches of today are liberal organizations that have very few similar qualities with the first-century church. Most resemble the church before Jesus rather than the church after Jesus' coming. Most attendees of church do not realize that if their righteousness does not exceed the leadership's righteousness, they will never see the Kingdom of God. You must be selfless. Our pastors are selfish and extremely poor role models, causing others to fall.

Our pastors are good men. Our pastors are good husbands and probably good friends. But are they godly men? Are they obedient men? Are they Christlike servants? Unfortunately, the fruit that their lives reveal says the world is their first love, just like the church at Ephesus. We are not to compare ourselves to the people around us, for then we are good. We are to compare our lives to God, Jesus, and Paul, who imitates Jesus.

God tells us we are to love Him, and then our neighbor, and then ourselves. We do God an injustice by stating that He has first place in our lives when our lives do not show it. We can all talk the talk, but it's our walk that people see and copy. As pastors and teachers, we cause others to believe that our way is acceptable. The only life acceptable to God is Jesus' life. We all must imitate Him. What does it mean to imitate Jesus? I put together a list of some of the attributes of Jesus using God's Word as the basis. We cannot do some of what we know about Jesus, like being born of a virgin. But we have access to the same power source. Unfortunately, because of our self-centeredness, we do not imitate Jesus in the ways we can and should. Remember, heaven is a free gift but our lives must indicate that God is in control because we want Him to be. Our lives must bear good fruit; causing others to fall short of obedience is not good fruit.

The following are things God tells us about Jesus, the one we are to imitate. He was:

- Single.
- Compassionate and caring.
- Holy—set apart.
- God in the flesh.
- Born of a virgin.
- Forgiving of sin.
- Approachable by anyone.
- Servant to all.
- Prayerful, humble, loving, sinless or pure, obedient, and patient.
- A teacher.
- The Word.
- Light.
- Salt.
- Truth.
- A healer.
- Gentle, meek, and kind.
- A provider.
- A counselor.
- Always at work.
- Faithful.
- Slow to anger.
- Gracious.
- Wise.
- A redeemer.
- A witness.
- A helper.
- Divine.
- Sovereign.
- A friend and brother.
- Fruit-bearing.
- Knowledge.

- Powerful.
- In Fear/Reverence for the Lord
- Delighted to be in the fear of the Lord.
- Righteous.
- Consistent.
- Persistent.
- A judge.
- A leader.
- Leader by example.
- Always in God's will, not His.

These are just some of the characteristics we know about Jesus from the Word of God. We also know Paul imitates Jesus, and we find these characteristics of Jesus by looking at Paul.

- Giver
- Does not hinder the gospel
- Sacrifice for God's will
- Testify
- Finds contentment
- Preaches God's word
- Passionate
- Works hard or is industrious
- Preaches for free

God gives us three individuals in His word who we should imitate. God says to imitate Him. God tells us to imitate Jesus. God also says to imitate Paul, who imitates Jesus. Each of us is called to die to self daily—actually moment to moment every day. Just as the Son of Man (Jesus) did not come to be served, but to serve, we are to serve, not self-serve. God says when we serve "the least of these," we serve Him. Even pagans serve (love) their families. God says in Philippians 2:3 "Regard one another as more important than yourselves."

You have had a pretty good look at the pastors at Chapel of the Flock Christian Church. They are an excellent example of where God said the church would be. That's probably why I had to write this book. The chairman of the Board of Elders once said to me, "The staff thinks this is a frat house." The pastors are seldom at church at any time. The receptionist, Francis Raleigh's wife, says they work from home. The associate pastor, David Scott, spends maybe twelve hours a week, Monday through Friday, at church. He never comes to a prayer service. He is the same pastor who wrote in the trail of messages, "As leaders, I think it is responsible on our part to make good disciples." David Scott wants to make good disciples; he just does not want to be one. Francis Raleigh is at church more than any of our other pastors by far. The sad part is, most of the congregation realizes they are seldom there. And many of them are seen during the day, gardening, mowing, and doing other things that validate that kind of dedication or lack of dedication. It may surprise you to find out that David Scott is the pastor in charge of the food pantry. He has never been seen at the food pantry.

David Scott also wrote in the trail of messages, "Other than scripture referring to members being of one body of Christ, there is no other directive in scripture that guides churches in how they should pursue membership in the local body." I believe God feels like His plan for membership is sufficient. Francis Raleigh and his associates believe God's plan for membership is "not adequate for what the person needs." I wonder what part of God's command, "Do not add or subtract from these words" these educated "pastors" cannot understand.

Jesus paid the penalty for all our sins, having cancelled the written code with its regulations that were against us and stood opposed to us. He took it away, nailing it to the cross. David Scott and his associates decided to add regulations back. It must be a post-crucifixion addition since God forgot to distinguish between His church and our church. I thought David Scott did a fine job of establishing Chapel of the Flock's pastor's position in regard to the Holy Spirit. Remember David wrote, "The 'down front' experience with decisions on Sunday morning is often not adequate for what the person needs." A message, hopefully from God's Word, is preached. The Holy Spirit of God moves on an individual. The individual makes a decision to say yes to God for whatever God is asking of him, and it is "not adequate"? David continues to write, "We do the best we can on the spot but I find the people that come forward need more than what we can give them at the moment." You see, it is all about *we* and *I*. David does not realize that God is sufficient. Nothing is impossible with God. God says, "He that is in you is sufficient to teach you all things. You need no man to teach you anything" (1 John 2:27). The fruit of their actions indicate to me the pastors do not believe in the presence of the Holy Spirit. I know by their actions or lack thereof, they do not fear Him. I believe in any case, the movement of the Holy Spirit and/or God's Word is secondary to their goals—in this case, tweaking the membership.

David Scott and his associates do not know that God is at work. Or they do not recognize God is at work. Or they do not believe God is at work. My personal belief is that tweaking the membership is an effort to get more work out of the membership for fear they may have to actually do something.

I believe what is wrong in the church today is because of poor leadership. We as pastors and teachers set poor examples of servant-hood. We are making disciples just like ourselves, who, in our current state of devotion to God, have no chance of entering heaven. When we participate in or condone adding to or subtracting from God's Word, we have put our eternity at risk. Setting mandatory classes with written contracts, establishing new laws, and denying the Holy Spirit is blaspheming. God says in Ezekiel 20:27, "Your fathers blasphemed me by forsaking me." Forsaking the Holy Spirit is blaspheming the Holy Spirit.

God gives us direction over and over and over throughout His Word: we are our brother's keeper. Today's social climate does not allow the open giving or accepting of criticism. However, we are responsible for each other: we, as pastors and teachers, even more so. That we are to warn one another is foundational in the Old and the New Testament. We are to warn one another not to sin against the Lord. Even not praying for someone is sinning against the Lord. Otherwise, God's wrath will come on you and your brothers. We are to help one another recognize the sin in our lives. In holding each other accountable, in love, we are also helping each other grow closer to God. As Christlike individuals, we must share openly our recognition of sin or be held accountable for the blood God will demand of a fellow Christian. We as pastors and teachers are rejecting God when our lives do not illustrate undivided devotion to the Lord, our God.

Mike Eaton wrote in the trail of messages: "More and more persons in our mobile society are moving frequently between different congregations for various reasons, and as a result are becoming less grounded doctrinally as well as spiritually." I think what Mike wrote is basically true. People are looking for something to fill the void God designed into every human being. People are searching for truth, which is Jesus. When a searcher recognizes lying, cheating, exploitation, laziness, misrepresentation of God's Word, dishonesty, and deceit, he will make the right choice and move on. God says, "Do not be misled: Bad company corrupts good character." People "becoming less grounded doctrinally as well as spiritually" is a teaching, preaching, and illustration problem. We must point people to Jesus and then walk the walk of servant-hood.

If we preach God's Word and we, the teachers and preachers, live lives that exhibit being within the parameters of God's Word, we will draw people, not repulse them. God does a wonderful job of telling us what to do and what not to do. He lists the dos and don'ts. We do not like to obey—never have, never will, outside of Jesus. The same problem has existed for over thirty-five hundred years. Every time God had to discipline His chosen people, it was because of their leaders.

"From the least to the greatest, all are greedy for gain; prophets and priests alike, all practice deceit" (Jeremiah 6:13).

"A horrible and shocking thing has happened in the land: The prophets prophesy lies, the priests rule by their own authority, and my people love it this way. But what will you do in the end?" (Jeremiah 5:30).

"But then they would flatter Him with their mouths, lying to Him with their tongues; their hearts were not loyal to Him, they were not faithful to His covenant" (Psalm 78:36).

"For the sins of their mouths, for the words of their lips let them be caught in their pride. For the curses and lies they utter" (Psalm 59:12).

"No one who practices deceit will dwell in my house; no one who speaks falsely will stand in my presence" (Psalm 101:7).

Our lives must indicate truth, honesty, integrity, and holiness. Misuse of God's Word cannot be tolerated by us, the people. God will not tolerate it. This is the very reason God cannot, nor will He, confirm His Word or gospel as He did in the first-century church. Francis Raleigh, on Sunday, August 21, 2011, gave us a fitting example of why God does not confirm His Word in the modern churches.

As I said earlier, James Cantrell, a mentor of Francis Raleigh, preached God had first place in his life. James also preached that his job or duties could not, nor should they, come before his wife or children. James always taught that the relationship between himself and his family was more important than the needs of the congregation. This applied to everyone on staff. Francis Raleigh has taught this same teaching as God's directive, as does James, his mentor. I have always felt this was inconsistent with God's Word but never felt led to address the subject.

On Sunday, August 21, 2011, Francis Raleigh said from the pulpit that pastors who spend a lot of time with and for their congregations while their wives and children struggle to have an appropriate relationship with them is a sin. Francis went on to tell us that certain of these individuals are out in the community doing this, and that the community thinks they are so "neat." Yet their family does not have enough time with them; this is a sin.

My twenty years of silence came to an end. God would not allow me to be silent any longer on an issue 180 degrees from His teaching. Francis calling a sin what God calls blessed would not fly. I wrote a letter of rebuttal to Francis and sent a copy to the chairman of the board. You would not believe the letter Francis wrote back to me. Francis proved to me you can be a pastor for thirty-five years and have very little understanding or knowledge of the Bible. Francis actually justified this teaching of his, not with scripture.

Francis taught from the pulpit that it was a sin to spend an excess amount of time helping others and not spend enough time with your wife or children. I have four sons and one daughter. Each one will tell you they did not get enough of my time. Each one will say one of the others got more. What is enough time? Looking at James Cantrell and Francis Raleigh and each of the pastors at Chapel of the Flock Christian Church, enough time is first place. Do you see a problem? We are to imitate God (Ephesians 5:1). God gave His Son as a ransom for others. The twelve apostles left everything to follow Jesus (Matthew 19:27).

"Jesus said to them, 'I tell you the truth, at the renewal of all things, when the Son of Man sits on His glorious throne, you who have followed me will also sit on twelve thrones, judging the twelve tribes of Israel. And everyone who has left houses or brothers or sisters or father or mother or children or fields for my sake will receive a hundred times as much and will inherit eternal life" (Matthew 19:28–29).

I also showed Francis this scripture: "Anyone who loves his father or mother more than me is not worthy of me; anyone who loves his son or daughter more than me is not worthy of me" (Matthew 10:37).

"If anyone comes to me and does not hate his father and mother, his wife and children, his brothers and sisters—yes, even his own life – he cannot be my disciple" (Luke 14:26).

"In the same way, any of you who does not give up everything he has cannot be my disciple"(Luke 14:33).

In Francis's letter back to me, he said I took these scriptures out of context. I also explained to Francis about Deuteronomy 33:8 and 9, where God, through Moses at the end of Moses's life, blesses the tribes of Israel. Here, God blesses the tribe of Levi for Aaron, who had no regard for his father or mother, did not recognize his brothers, and did not acknowledge his children, but watched over God's Word and covenant. God has first place in Francis Raleigh's life right after his family, and Francis's congregation sees, believes, and responds in like manner. Therefore six to twenty-five attend Wednesday night prayer services.

All Christians are to imitate God, imitate Jesus, and imitate Paul, who imitates Jesus. Jesus is our benchmark. We, as pastors and teachers, are obligated by God to those we are supposed to be serving. We must be windows through which Jesus is seen. We cannot continue to set poor examples of a Christlike life. Many people do not know the Bible or Jesus. The only Bible they receive is what they hear from us. The only Jesus they see is what they see in us.

We cannot continue to play church without God's presence. We can do nothing without Him. We talk about His presence because Jesus told us, "Where two or more come together in my name, there I am with them." Jesus also tells us in the previous verse, "If two ask for anything in my name it will be done." Why do we not have what we ask for? God wants to heal our sick and lame. What is wrong? Jesus explains the answer in Matthew 21:21 and 22. Jesus says, "If you have faith and do not doubt." He also says, "If you believe, you will receive whatever you ask for in prayer." The reasons God does not answer our prayers are the same reasons He does not confirm His message as He did before the alliance of the church and the world. We do not believe or have faith. We do have doubt. The pastors of Chapel of the Flock made public their position in the "trail of messages." Did they ever mention God the Father or God the Son or the Holy Spirit in response to the lady's questions? They responded, "We find, we do, I find, we would, we have, I can, or we can." God's leading presence is not recognized nor will God ever confirm a message that is not His.

In the past, God overlooked such ignorance, but now He commands all people everywhere to repent. God is unchanging. Throughout four thousand years of God-revealed history, God has told us to be holy for He is holy—set apart. God has warned and disciplined His chosen people about making alliances with the world. He wants us to put our trust and faith in Him. God tells us, "Friendship with the world is hatred toward Him." This unchanging God said it like this three thousand years ago in 2 Chronicles 15:2, "The Lord is with you when you are with Him. If you seek Him, He will be found by you, but if you forsake Him, He will forsake you."

Have we forsaken God? God does not confirm His message as He did in the early church. God gives us directives throughout His Word. God gives promises if we obey His commands, if we put these commands into practice. The commands are very simple: love God with all your heart, with all your soul, and with all your strength; and love your neighbor as yourself. Notice the word *all*. God uses the word *all* so Francis Raleigh will understand not with your wife or not with your children. God wants, and more importantly, deserves, all your love. Francis Raleigh taught on August 21, 2011, this is a sin. Has Francis Raleigh forsaken God? How about his staff and elders who go along with this teaching? How about the twelve hundred attendees who witness this message and remain silent, or worse yet, see no wrong? Have we forsaken God for the world?

God told His chosen people, "Obey me." God told His people through Moses over thirty-five hundred years ago (Exodus 15:26), "If you listen carefully to the voice of the Lord your God and do what is right in His eyes, if you pay attention to His commands and keep all His decrees, I will not bring on you any of the diseases I brought on the Egyptians, for I am the Lord who heals you." God gave them miraculous sign after miraculous sign, including His presence, and they forsook Him. God disciplined them with forty years in the desert until the entire generation that forsook Him had died.

God brought His chosen people into the promised land with miracle after miracle. Before entering the promised land, God told them to eliminate the living cancer there and to not make alliances with the people so they would not be infected. They disobeyed. The cancer infected them. God sent messengers to His chosen people, telling them to repent of their cancer or He would disperse them out of their country for seventy years. They disobeyed. God made good on His promise. God told His people after seventy years, He would relent on His anger and return the remnant of His people to the promised land. God brought His people back after seventy years when Cyrus, king of Persia, in his first year as king, sent them to Jerusalem to rebuild the temple as Jeremiah had said God would. But the sin of the priests and elders leading the people astray into alliances with the world brought more discipline. The chosen people were dispersed again until 1948.

God describes these alliances of His people and the world in several different places in the Bible. The one in Ezekiel 23 I like because God calls Samaria *Oholah* and calls Jerusalem *Oholibah*—adulterous sisters. God says Oholah engaged in prostitution while she was still His. God calls them both prostitutes because they did not keep themselves holy (set apart) but rather entered into an alliance with the world. God says in Ezekiel 23:35, "Therefore this is what the Sovereign Lord says: Since you have forgotten me and thrust me behind your back, you must bear the consequences of your lewdness and prostitution." The point is, through four thousand years of Biblical history, God has directed us to be set apart from the world.

God wants us to trust and obey Him as a result of our total love and devotion for Him because He first loved us completely. We fail Him and deserve the punishment Jesus has already taken in our place. Fortunately, God does not give us what we deserve yet. He takes pity on us and relents from His anger. God continues to reach out to us through dreams, visions, and preaching. God speaks to each and every person in this world. He does not want anyone to be apart from Him for eternity but He leaves that decision up to each one of us. Most people do not hear Him. Some hear Him but ignore what He has to say while others convince themselves it is not God but their conscience or imagination. Saying no to God is habitual for most of us.

Christians must be attentive to God's speaking. We must bring Him into the middle of everything we do through prayer. Remember, we can do nothing without Him. God cannot afford to allow us to be successful without Him. We would be even more prideful as well as become hardened of heart, which would ensure our destruction. We have to stay within the parameters He sets for us because when we do not, we are rejecting Him. If we seek Him, we will find Him. If we reject Him, He will reject us.

My wife and I live in the Bible belt. We have visited many congregations, and I have studied with evangelists from other denominations. There are at least one hundred churches within twenty minutes of our house. Chapel of the Flock Christian Church is as good as or better than any we have visited or heard about. Our messages each week are from the Bible. We read scripture at different times during the service. We put scripture on the overhead screens during the service as well.

We at Chapel of the Flock Christian Church have great intentions, but like most modern churches, each of our leaders is in love with his life. Our leaders are bathed in the world. There is no fruit that speaks of self-denial. Most of our sermons are right on; you cannot find fault with them. But once every four to six weeks, way too often, our leadership tries to sell some ridiculous story. It is widely spoken that preachers and teachers use illustrations that are not true because they fit their message. Saying something that is not true is a lie. I do not agree with James Cantrell. The end does not justify the means. God is all about the means. He takes care of the end. I believe God, who says all lies come from the father of lies, the devil. No lie comes from the truth and the truth will have no part with the one who lies. Changing God's Word, however expertly done, will result in punishment—if not in this life, in the next.

I am sure if you are on guard for it, you will find the same deceit in your local body. God warns us throughout His Word, do not be deceived— do not deceive ourselves or each other. We should know the truth, not allowing ourselves to be deceived. The purity of God's Word is our responsibility and we are to test everything with it.

To illustrate deception from the pulpit, I am going to give you a few examples from Chapel of the Flock's messages. I gave one earlier where Francis said pastors who are devoted to others rather than their wives and children are sinners. That would make God a sinner because He placed others before His Son, even to death on a cross.

We had a sermon series recently from 1 Corinthians. The message from 1 Corinthians 7 was that Pastor Francis was a better man because of his wife. She made him more complete. The message of 1 Corinthians 7 is all about not getting married, if possible, in order to give God our undivided attention. I do not know how anyone can preach 1 Corinthians 7 and say the message is that he is a better man because of his wife and let it go at that. Truly, she does make him more complete, a better man. She is a help mate. God says in 1 Corinthians 7:1, "It is good for a man not to marry." God also states that because there is so much immorality, each man should have his own wife. God says in verse 6 that He would rather all men were like Paul, single. He allows us to marry as a concession. God created Eve for Adam, and she ushered in sin and changed creation forever.

"I would like you to be free from concern. An unmarried man is concerned about the Lord's affairs – how he can please the Lord. But a married man is concerned about the affairs of this world – how he can please his wife and his interests are divided. An unmarried woman or virgin is concerned about the Lord's affairs: Her aim is to be devoted to the Lord in both body and spirit. But a married woman is concerned about the affairs of this world – how she can please her husband. I am saying this for your own good, not to restrict you, but that you may live in a right way in *undivided devotion to the Lord*" (1 Corinthians 7:32–35).

I know this is difficult for people. My wife, who is sharp and has understanding, struggles with it. Grasp the fact, God is beyond our understanding. He deserves our undivided love and devotion and He expects it. Marriage is the start of worldly living (verse 33). Remember James 4:4: "You adulterous people, don't you know that friendship with the world is hatred toward God? Anyone who chooses to be a friend of the world becomes an enemy of God."

God must have first place in our lives. He does not want to share first place, nor will He.

On another Sunday, while preaching from 1 Corinthians 14, Francis was trying to downplay the importance of speaking in tongues. Francis said if anyone is speaking in tongues, it must be an understandable language. He said it must be a language such as French, Russian, German, or whatever. Francis said it cannot be something no one understands. Francis went on to say it must be interpreted. We know in Acts 2 there were many different languages present and each person heard the message being spoken from the 120 speaking in tongues in his own language. But here in 1 Corinthians 14:2, God says, "For anyone who speaks in tongues does not speak to men but to God. Indeed, *no one understands him*, he utters mysteries with his spirit." Francis, while teaching and preaching 1 Corinthians 14, teaches something 180 degrees from what the Bible says.

A few weeks ago, giving was down, so Francis gave us a couple of sermons on the subject. He said in one that Jesus preached more about the giving of money than any other one topic. Francis said, "Isn't it ironic that the only time the writer of the book of Acts quotes Jesus, it is about giving money?" Francis then read Acts 20:35d: "It is more blessed to give than to receive." If we look at Acts chapter 20, verses 33, 34, and 35, we find the author, God through Luke, writes quoting Paul in 33. Paul says he has not "coveted anyone's silver or gold or clothing." Francis, in an effort to obtain silver and gold, is using this area of scripture. Paul goes on to say his hands have supplied for the needs of himself and his companions. Paul tell us in verse 35 that he is showing us by this kind of hard work that we must help the weak. Then Paul quotes Jesus. The giving here is not silver or gold, although sometimes money fits the need. The giving as illustrated is giving of self, self-sacrifice, the denying of self in service to others.

Again, Francis said from the pulpit, "The only time the writer of the book of Acts quotes Jesus, it is about money." Jesus is quoted in Acts 9:4; in Acts 7:10; in Acts 9:11, 15, 16; in Acts 11:16; in Acts 18:9, 10; in Acts 22:7, 8, 18, 21; in Acts 23:11; as well as Acts 26:14, 15, 16, 17 and 18. God says, "Do not be deceived." Gold fever is a well-documented disease and not all prospectors are in the hills of California.

A few months ago, while preaching on Luke 19:1–10, Francis Raleigh told us that Zachaeus was a liar, a cheat, and a thief. Francis said, "Zacchaeus became rich cheating other Jews while collecting taxes." God says in Luke 19:1–10 that Zacchaeus was a chief tax collector. God says in those passages that Zacchaeus was wealthy. God never states that Zacchaeus was a liar or a cheat nor does He say he was a thief. In fact, God says just the opposite. That is right, 180 degrees of what Francis is preaching. God's Word says in verse 8 that Zacchaeus here and now gave half of his possessions to the poor. Zacchaeus goes on to say, "If I have cheated anybody out of anything, I will pay back four times the amount." God is telling us a truth using mathematics. If Zacchaeus had $1 million, he gave half to the poor ($500,000). Francis said Zacchaeus became wealthy cheating his countrymen. He got to be a millionaire cheating people. *If* Zacchaeus cheated people to get $1 million, how could he give four times that amount back? He now only has $500,000. Francis is right in his accusations, but not about Zacchaeus. The listeners of these false statements, do they share in the guilt? Is silence acceptable when God's Word is involved?

Like most churches in the years 2008 and 2009, giving started falling off dramatically. Money became tight at church and in individuals' homes. People were losing their jobs, their savings, their homes, as well as their peace, unfortunately. Finance was so bad at Chapel of the Flock Christian Church that Francis did a seven-week series on giving. As he always does, Francis set a structure as to how often and how much we should give. Francis likes using 1 Corinthians 16:2 as a foundation for giving 10 percent of your gross earnings before taxes each week.

I do not want to change the way anyone gives to God. I do not want to set any standards. I do desire that we use God's Word to the best of our ability in teaching God's desires. I do not say giving each Sunday is wrong or right. It seems to work. Francis also always uses 2 Corinthians 9:5b and 9:7 to build on the ten percent of gross income weekly foundation. If I understand God correctly, all who listen to these messages and remain silent share in the guilt.

God tells us through Paul in 1 Corinthians 16:2 to set aside a sum of money in keeping with our income so that when Paul comes, "no collections" will have to be made. Paul in verse 6 is going to stay a while, maybe all winter. Paul wants "no collections" to be made when he comes. This is a onetime gift for the saints in Jerusalem talked about in several places in the Bible. The collection and giving of this gift has been over a year in coming. Paul even sends other brothers ahead of himself to ensure the gift is ready so he will not be embarrassed, because Paul has been "boasting" about this gift since last year (2 Corinthians 9:1–3).

Paul never wanted to be around the collection of money. Paul did not want the gospel message hindered in any way. Paul even preached for free. We know a worker deserves his wages. Paul says he has a right to such help, but *we* did not use this right because they did not want to hinder the gospel of Christ (1 Corinthians 9:12). Paul also told us he worked night and day, laboring and toiling, not because they did not have a right to be paid, but "in order to make ourselves a model for you to follow." We are to imitate God the Father, God the Son, and Paul, who imitates Jesus. How far off is the modern church?

Francis, with our chairman of the board of elders, David Manuel, did a two-man skit during the seven-week sermon series. They used Malachi 3:8 and Malachi 3:10 in telling the listeners that we were robbing God by not tithing—giving 10 percent of your gross income before taxes. I have been in the church for nearly thirty years. The only thing I have ever heard a message from Malachi on is tithing 10 percent and robbing God. Malachi is a short book consisting of only four chapters. Malachi is primarily about the wickedness of priests. I urge you to read it and pay particular attention to 3:18, especially you, Francis and David.

Hebrews 7:5 reads, "Now the law requires the descendants of Levi who become priests to collect a tenth from the people." Colossians 2:13 and 14 read, "When you were dead in your sins and in uncircumcision of your sinful nature, God made you alive with Christ. He forgave us our sins, having cancelled the written code, with its regulations, that was against us and that stood opposed to us; He took it away, nailing it to the cross."

I will talk more about tithing later, but I want to give you some information to hopefully rev your motor. God gave us the law of tithing through Moses over thirty-five hundred years ago. God is unchanging. Why should He change? He is flawless in word and deed. God wants each of us to have a personal, one-on-one relationship with Him. This was true thirty-five hundred years ago and this is true today. God wants us to come to Him. God had Moses write the first five books of the Bible for our instruction. God instructs us in these five books to bring our sacrifices for Him, to Him. He does not want us worshiping Him outside His presence, especially as a matter of convenience (Leviticus 17:3, 4, 5, 8, and 9). The law of the tithe is for one-tenth of everything. One-tenth of everything belongs to the Lord (Leviticus 27:30–32). Always know God wants and deserves to be revered. He calls for us to revere Him, and He has set the laws of the Old Testament so that when we obey them, we will revere Him. God explains clearly in Deuteronomy 12:5, 6, 7, 12, 13, 17, 18 the tithe, the 10 percent that is holy to the Lord: you are to eat that tithe in the presence of the Lord. God is even more distinctly clear in Deuteronomy 14:22–29 as to whom, where, why, and how much is the tithe. God explains, "You and your household shall eat there in the presence of Lord your God and rejoice." God explains clearly the tithe of years one and two are your own in the presence of the Lord. You are not giving the tithe away; you and your household are consuming it in God's presence. The tithe of the third year goes to the Levites and other needs (charities). In truth, your donation to the church is 3 1/3 percent to the church. It's actually less if the church is not looking after the aliens, the fatherless, and the widows. God again repeats these instructions in Deuteronomy 26:12 and 13. Why does church leadership not teach these truths? The same reason they do not imitate Paul, who preached for free as a model for us to follow (2 Thessalonians 3:9).

God gives us an illustration of how He feels about priests who want a portion of every year's tithe! Read 1 Samuel 2. You will find the place where the Lord has His name is Shiloh. The priests there are Eli and his two sons, Hophni and Phinehas. Hophni and Phinehas are helping themselves to every year's tithe, not just the third year. In verse 29, God calls it "fattening yourselves" of "every offering." Eli, Hophni, and Phinehas all lose their lives over it—as well, the curse is carried on to their posterity. I suggest you read 1 Samuel 1–3 to see all that happens, but chapter 2 is where God addresses the theft.

We only know what God tells us in His Word and what we see in His creation. Why do we as pastors and teachers risk eternity with God for the pleasures of this life—a life that has the value of one grain of sand on the beach of eternity? We have the opportunity to serve an unimaginable, awesome God. He wants to give us life abundantly, beyond our imaginations, but we choose to ignore Him, cheat Him, and change His words, which are flawless, so we can lead lazy, fruitless lives.

God tells us what He will do if we obey Him, and He explains what He will do if we choose not to obey. God has done this for thirty-five hundred years, over and over, and we continue to try Him out. We talked about it before: throughout Israel's history, their priests have perverted the Word of God, leading the people astray, including crucifying Jesus. With all the discipline God delivered to Israel, He says the priests and prophets lie and His people like it this way. We as human beings like to deceive, and we like to be deceived. The fruit of our lives indicate this is true—in church, in government, and in how we live our lives.

Unfortunately, the social climate of today is such that everyone can do their own thing. It dictates if a person desires to be unnatural in their sexual relations, not only should we permit it, we should openly condone it. God calls this unnatural activity "indecent acts" (Romans 1:27). God says these "shameful lusts," which are acts of "sexual impurity," are a lie and shall not be committed (Romans 1:27). God also tells us that we must not "associate" with a person such as this, who calls himself a Christian (1 Corinthians 5:11).

Each of us will be held responsible if we condone this type of behavior. Silence is condoning. Today we as a nation not only condone this activity, we promote it as an acceptable behavior. Therefore we are calling God a liar. My concern is not so much for the person involved in these unnatural relations, although I am concerned, as I am concerned for those of us who approve of this activity through silence or distancing ourselves from it. Distancing ourselves from it is a good idea but we cannot be silent on the subject, even in staying away from those involved. Always leave room for repentance. Be ready to forgive in all cases; in all situations "love the sinner but hate the sin." God is quite clear in 1 Corinthians 6:9–10 where He says, "Do you not know that the wicked will not inherit the kingdom of God? Do not be deceived: Neither the sexually immoral nor idolaters nor adulterers nor male prostitutes nor homosexual offenders nor thieves nor the greedy nor drunkards nor slanderers nor swindlers will inherit the kingdom of God."

I understand being tolerant of someone's open sin seems like a good thing. And I think we all practice it to some degree but God calls us to be straight-up with a person. For instance, I have a couple who I am close to. They live together, not married. They have lived together for about two years. They are great workers in the church. They come to prayer meetings and serve on various service teams. They are more committed to serving others than 90 percent of the church membership. I baptized Matt last Saturday. I talked with him about his responsibility as a baptized believer. He said he did not want to be a role model. I told him it did not matter what he wanted to be in that area. After you are baptized, you are not only a role model but you are a witness for Christ and a co-heir with Jesus as well. My hope is that he will make the right decision on his own and not need my prompting.

We were looking at what God tells us in 1 Corinthians 6:9–10. Take note of thieves, the greedy, slanderers, and swindlers. Have you ever been swindled or stolen from? We normally think in terms of finance when we think of these things. I would like to revisit the trail of messages. David Scott, associate pastor, is concerned about the expectations and requirements for being Christlike.

I feel safe in saying that what is most profound about Jesus' life is His servant-hood and obedience. Jesus was obedient to His Father even to death on a cross. Paul is most emphatic about not hindering the gospel. Knowing we are to imitate Jesus and imitate Paul, who imitates Jesus, these three qualities should be evident in our lives. That is, our lives should exhibit servant-hood, obedience to God, and we should in no way hinder the gospel. God uses Paul to illustrate for us how not to hinder the gospel.

God tells us a person preaching the gospel should be paid for his labor. God also tells us if others have this right, should not Paul have it "all the more?" Paul says he does not use this right because he does not want to hinder the gospel. How is Paul not hindering the gospel by preaching the gospel for free? Paul asks the question, "Is it only I and Barnabus who must work for a living?" Paul says he worked harder than any of the other apostles. God tells us through Paul in Philippians 4:9: "Whatever you have learned or received or heard from me, or seen in me—put it into practice." Are these just words? Is God serious?

God says through Paul in 1 Thessalonians 2:9: "Surely you remember brothers, our toil and hardship; we worked night and day in order not to be a burden to anyone while we preached the gospel of God to you." God repeats that message in 2 Thessalonians 3:7-9: "For you yourselves know how you ought to follow our example. We were not idle when we were with you, nor did we eat anyone's food without paying for it. On the contrary, we worked night and day, laboring and toiling so that we would not be a burden to any of you. We did this, not because we do not have the right to such help, but in order to make ourselves a model for you to follow."

God does not use James or Jude, Jesus' brothers, as models for us to follow. God does not give examples of Peter or John or Phillip for us to imitate. God uses Paul, who will do anything to not tarnish the message he has been asked to preach. God, over and over throughout the New Testament uses Paul as our model, our example, the one who imitates Jesus. Something has been left out in application of God's Word in the modern church. At Chapel of the Flock Christian Church, we have nine ordained ministers. We cannot get them to prayer meetings, let alone get them to work outside the church or preach for free.

David Scott, who in the trail of messages was so zealously concerned about expectations and requirements of being Christlike, is extremely hard to find. The fact is, Pat and Jenny, who worked the food pantry for nine years say they never saw David Scott at the food pantry. I have been told by those still working the food pantry that David has not been there in the last ten years. It is part of his job. I would think anyone so concerned about what it means to be Christlike would desire to exhibit those traits of servant-hood, obedience, and live a life such as to not hinder the gospel. Rather, David has earned the nickname of Casper.

I believe from what I have witnessed in nearly thirty years in the church, Chapel of the Flock Christian Church is like all the churches. The fact that we have not had one elder or one pastor at our food pantry in ten years is the truth and a shame. Hindering the gospel was

a concern for Paul and was and is for God. For today's pastors, it is part
of the job description.

You have been given a pretty good look at Chapel of the Flock Christian
Church's leadership. I want to again emphasize that our leaders are
good men. When you compare our elders and pastors to the men of
this world, our leaders are at the top. When you compare them to Paul
or Jesus, there are very few similarities. Our leaders are so deep in the
world, if they did not speak (tell you they are Christians), you could not
distinguish them from any good man outside Jesus. Remember, Jesus
said, "He who does not gather with me, scatters."

We can no longer wait on leadership to lead by example. It will not
happen. It has not happened in the over thirty-five hundred year history
of God's chosen people. We are part of that family of chosen people if
we are circumcised of the heart by the Spirit. Our lives must indicate
we have accepted God's grace and mercy and are eternally thankful.
God must have first place in our lives. God must have our undivided
devotion. Putting your spouse and your children before God is not
what God considers first place. This teaching breeds acceptance of
that idea, and the result is you are scattering, not gathering for the
kingdom.

Alliance

I am going to step out on a limb. I do not want to offend anyone or any organization. I only want what God wants. I want no one to perish, especially my personal family and friends. But perish we will if we continue to walk with one leg in the world and one leg in the family of God. We need to be committed to one another. We have to direct each other's focus to Jesus the Christ, who is our benchmark.

I was taught in school that when Rome accepted Christianity, it was a glorious day. It was a new era for Christianity. No longer would Christians be fed to wild animals; no longer would Christians be nailed to crosses; no longer would Christians be slaughtered in the arena. These realities are good in and of themselves, that is, no more harsh treatment. But look back over the last two thousand years: these harsh treatment realities are true. What has been the cost? Does God confirm His message of the gospel the way He did before the alliance between the church and the world? God tells us He is *unchanging*. God says in Hebrews 13:8, "Jesus Christ is the same yesterday and today and forever." If God is unchanging, what has changed that God would no longer confirm His message?

Two very important changes have been made. First, the message is no longer God's message. You have looked at a few subtle changes in God's message from Francis Raleigh. Remember, on August 21, 2011, Francis Raleigh preached that it is a sin to spend more time with the members of your congregation than you do with your wife and children, as some pastors do. Yet God says we are to imitate Him (Ephesians 5:1). God did not spare His own Son, but gave Him up for us all (Romans 8:32). God also says in Romans 14:16, "Do not allow what you consider good to be spoken of as evil." Jesus said He came to serve, not to be served. Service to others is good, as illustrated by Jesus in His obedience to God. God calls it righteousness and Francis calls it sin. Changing God's message then is one important change, and of course God will not confirm a message that is not His. The other change that God will not tolerate is His people making an alliance with the people of the world.

God is unchanging; this we all know. God has stated His position in regard to His people making treaties or alliances with the people of the world, beginning during the Exodus from Egypt (Exodus 34:12). Each time the chosen people of God were disciplined severely by God, it was a direct result of their disobedience and their making an alliance with the people around them. Why would God change and promote this marriage of the church and the world, which is Rome? Look at the last seventeen to eighteen hundred years since the marriage. The good news is that God's Word has been kept pure and God will not allow His Word, the Bible, to be contaminated or changed. God says, "Heaven and earth will pass away, but my words will never pass away" (Matthew 24:35). We have the Bible to gain the knowledge of right and wrong. Friendship with the world is wrong.

Whether an alliance between the king of Judah, Jehoshaphat, and the king of Israel, Ahab, who was evil, God does not promote or condone His people making treaties with the worldly. At this time, Israel, Samaria, was outside God's will. Ahab was a wicked king. Everything that was written in the past was written to teach us (Romans 15:4). You see, God has given us this information so we can make correct decisions. God has given us these various illustrations to teach us that alliances (or treaties) with the world are not acceptable. If you will take the time to read 2 Chronicles, chapters 18 and 19, you find God describing a treaty that He does not condone. After Ahab was killed, God said to Jehoshaphat, king of Judah, "Should you help the wicked and love those who hate the Lord? Because of this, the wrath of the Lord is upon you." Actually, God said this through Jehu, the seer.

There is absolutely no way the church can have an alliance with the world and be in God's will. Read your Bible. Please, prove me wrong. In this statement from God through Jehu to Jehoshaphat, the word we translate to "love" in English actually can be translated "make alliance with." Do not take my word for it. Prove me wrong. Do not be deceived. Not by me, not by your pastor, not by someone masquerading as an angel of light.

Throughout the Old and New Testaments, God gives illustrations and commands to not be part of the world. We are to be in the world but not of the world. We are not to be friends of the world. How can we justify the marriage of the church and the world, which at this time was Rome? I do not think we can, from God's point of view, Biblically. When we look at this joining together from a human standpoint or from a social or worldly view, it seems sweet.

When we look back over the last two thousand years to where the church was in relation to God and then look century by century to where the church of God was and where it is, we see deception by he who masquerades as the angel of light. Praise God! He keeps His word pure and has made it readily available to us so we can test everything. Each of us is responsible for our own salvation. Each of us must appear before the judgment seat of Christ. We will receive what is due us, whether good or bad. Does God have first place in your life? Do you love Him with all your heart? Do you live a life in obedience to God? Francis Raleigh's preaching will not be an excuse. Do you try to live a good life in your eyes? Do you do what you want? Are you better than the guy next door? Jesus lived a life of service. Is Jesus your benchmark?

God is quite clear that most people will not go to heaven, few will. Yes, many people will go to heaven. But when you compare the numbers, most will not be with God for eternity. Heaven is a free gift from God. We must accept the gift and live lives that reflect the fact that we have repented and are serving in thanksgiving. Heaven is our choice. We can say yes to Jesus or spend eternity apart from God, which is a terrible choice.

Do not allow the world or the effects of this world to hinder you. The world is a trap set by the prince of this world, Satan. God has given us two main weapons in the fight against the world and its leader: the Bible and prayer. With prayer, we can bring God into the middle of whatever we are involved in. Prayer is as essential as reading and studying God's Word. I suggest praying before every time you read the Bible. Ask God to open your mind and heart to what He has for you. Remember, it is God who says that if you seek Him, He will be found by you. God wants this personal relationship with you, and you want that same relationship with God, even if you do not know it. You were designed that way. God is the only one who can fill that need or void in your life.

There are many examples of God giving us directions in His Word. One of my favorites is 2 Chronicles 7:14–15. Here God shows how simple and easy it is to be within His will. Our initial problem is we have to get off the throne of our lives. We must discard the "me" syndrome. The world has a great problem with the "me" syndrome—that is, everything is about *me*. God tells us at the beginning of 2 Chronicles 7:14–15 to whom He is talking, "If my people, who are called by my name." First, God tells us to humble ourselves, get off the throne. Second, He says pray, draw Him near. Third, God says to seek His face, read His word—gather with other believers, desire God's presence. Fourth, God says we must turn from our wicked ways of not serving Him. God asks four simple things of us. Then He will forgive our sins and heal. Here the Word actually reads "heal our land." Could our land use healing? Twenty million people are out of work. Of those who are working, most are working for less.

The Occupy Wall Street movement has erupted from this need of healing. The media says this movement has no singular message, which it needs to be a real political threat. Our foundational problem is the deception throughout our society, in church, government, and our everyday life; thus our need for healing. I would like for us to look at 2 Chronicles 7:15. God says, "Now my eyes will be open and my ears attentive to the prayers offered in this place." First, to those who shy away from corporate prayer: God desires His House to be called a house of prayer. We use Matthew 18:20: "For where two or three come together in My name, there I am with them," to know God is with us when we meet in our services. But if you look at 20:18–19, Jesus is talking about corporate prayer. Second, look at the first word in 2 Chronicles 7:15, *now*. Does this suggest to you that God is not listening to those who do not humble themselves, pray, seek Him, and turn from their selfishness? God says throughout His Word that He does not listen to the disobedient, except when they repent and turn from their selfishness.

God desires us to revere Him as He knows we should. He wants us to accept His grace and mercy and turn from our selfishness and respond in thanksgiving by living lives of obedience. It is beyond my comprehension how anyone can believe this awesome creator of the world will allow individuals to spend eternity with Him in heaven who desired to spend no time with Him in this life. Heaven would then be just like this world. If you seek the truth, you will find it. It is your eternity; make the right choice.

I told you about the first two preaching pastors I served under. I made you aware of their deception and lies. I told you about James Cantrell, how he habitually lied in order to build a "Christian school." As well, he promoted service to family before service to others and called that God having first place.

One Sunday many years ago, probably eleven or twelve years ago, James Cantrell was preaching a sermon from Matthew 7:21–23. I was sitting in the third row directly in front of James.

"Not everyone who says to me, 'Lord, Lord', will enter the kingdom of heaven, but only he who does the will of my Father who is in heaven. Many will say to me on that day, 'Lord, Lord,' did we not prophesy in Your name, and in Your name drive out demons and perform many miracles?" (Matthew 7:21).

If you drove out demons and performed many miracles, God was working through you mightily. These are people God is utilizing in a big way. Matthew 7:23 says, "Then I will tell them plainly, I never knew you. Away from me, you evildoers!"

God spoke to me so plainly, not audibly, but He made me know that James Cantrell was preaching a message about himself. I sat through the entire sermon with tears flowing down my cheeks, nearly sobbing. I was made aware this man, for whatever motives, repeatedly lied to his flock, and he was going to have hell to pay for it. It broke my heart. Sometime later, James and I had a conversation about his repeatedly telling the congregation the $12 million building campaign had nothing to do with the school when in fact it was all about the school.

We in the church today justify lying or other wrongdoing if our motives are good—good in our own eyes. All lies are from the father of lies, the devil. There is no justification for them. Any wrongdoing by leadership in the church is an act of scattering, not gathering.

As you continue to read this book, I hope you are driven back to the Bible. I will repeat myself often when it comes to God's Word. Please pray and read and study the Bible. Reading God's Word is more important than reading anything else. Each of us must seek a relationship with God. Our eternity and the eternity of our children, grandchildren, and great-grandchildren depend on someone breaking from the tradition of worldly living.

God gives us another illustration about how He feels about worldly living in the book of Ezra. During the reign of King Artaxerxes, the people are returning to Judah from Babylon after seventy years of deportation. The people of Israel had not kept themselves separate from the peoples of the land. Including the priest and Levites, the people had intermarried with the Canaanites, Hittites, Perizzites, Jebusites, Ammonites, Moabites, Egyptians, and Amorites. Remember, we talked about God commanding Israel to kill every living thing in the land as they entered the promised land. God told Israel to eliminate what would end up a cancer for them. God told Israel not to intermarry with them.

Ezra prays to God in chapter 9, confessing the sins of the people, and Ezra is asking God for direction to remove their "great guilt" and punishment. Read Ezra 9 and 10 and discover for yourself how God feels about treaties with the world. We all know God does not like divorce. In this situation (treaties with the world), God has the Israelites send the wives and children away and names the guilty men by name. They are logged forever in God's Word (Ezra 10:18–44). How does this action fit Francis Raleigh's preaching to spend more time with your children and wife than serving God? God says in Ezra, chapter 9, "Do not seek a treaty of friendship with them at any time."

Again, Romans 15:4 says that everything that was written in the past was written to teach us. God has the prophet Ezekiel prophesy against Samaria and Jerusalem in Chapter 23 of Ezekiel. The entire chapter 23 is about two sisters, Oholah, who is Samaria, and Oholibah, who is Jerusalem (verse 4).

God is expressing Himself and showing His feelings as to what happens when His people have an alliance with those around them (the rest of the world). God calls it prostitution. When you have treaties, there are cultural exchanges that are a cancer to a people who are called to be holy or set apart. God calls His people to be holy as He is holy— separate from the world. We ignore all God's teachings when we call an alliance between the world, Rome, and the church good.

How can we Biblically justify the marriage between Rome and the church? We just looked at the book of Ezra. God nullified the marriages of the Israelites with the people around them and sent the children resulting from these marriages away as well. What did God have Abraham do with Ishmael? God said, "Listen to whatever Sarah tells you because it is through Isaac that your offspring will be reckoned." Sarah said, "Get rid of that slave woman and her son." Can you see why the leaders discourage reading the Bible for yourself? Does this help you understand why the church killed the men who translated the Bible into their own language, such as English?

When we think with God's Word as our foundation for thought, the marriage of the church and the world was not nor is it good. God demands complete separation. Our modern churches are children of that marriage. We, the church of today, are so liberal. The influence of the world saturates today's church, and unfortunately we are making disciples who believe this is how it should be.

Chapel of the Flock Christian Church is but an example, and as I said earlier, a much better example than most churches. Sadly, most of the members of Chapel of the Flock Christian Church, by the fruit of their lives, will never see the kingdom of heaven. Jesus will make that decision as to each of our eternal destinies. But Jesus will not judge; He will assay our lives and report what they dictate. Our leadership at Chapel of the Flock Christian Church is developing disciples similar to themselves. They talk the talk, but the walk tells another story. God is important in their lives but there are others things more important, such as wives, children, and free time.

The people of today are just like the people of two thousand or three thousand years ago. We sin the same. We think in the same manner as the previous generations: selfishly. We reject God's calling. We attempt to pervert God's desires. We have been warned by God just as they were warned. God warned the previous generations of His chosen people. They refused to listen, so they paid the price. God has warned us, and He has told us what the penalty for disobedience will be. We have over fifteen hundred years of history written and saved for our access. We have no excuse. The work has been done. The price has been paid. But we must accept the gift and live lives of thanksgiving. Our lives must say, "Thank you, Lord, for the hope you have given me through the efforts of Jesus." Neither you nor I can accept the hollow and deceptive philosophy, which depends on human tradition and the basic principles of this world rather than on Christ. No excuses will be accepted; we either *trust* and *obey* or we receive second death, which is hell.

I hope you took note of the origin and growth of the English Bible diagram at the beginning of this book. A conversation I had with a person very close to me made me realize this diagram needed to be not only in this book but near the front. She made a statement that many people went to heaven before the Bible was written. I did not try to justify my complete belief in the Bible because she is of a faith where traditionally the congregants do not read the Bible. The Bible is read by the leader and he tells the congregants what it says and what it means. This avenue of thought is not consistent with her personality. That is allowing someone else to tell her the correct train of thought and what is and is not. In most things, she would investigate herself, form an opinion, and be rigid in that opinion. She is rigid in her opinion, but the foundation for it is the tradition of her religion. Of course, she does not read the Bible because if she did, she would be leaving her current form of worshiping Jesus. Here is a woman with a big heart, a giving heart. If I asked her today for $25,000, she and her husband would give it to me. Notice I did not say borrow. If I told them I needed $25,000, they would give it to me. They would hope I would pay it back but it would not be a prerequisite. They both work. They do not make a lot of money. This is the type of people they are. God is important to them. But God is not a member of their first five. He is not part of the starting line-up. Their religion promotes this kind of thinking and so does mine if you watch the leadership and use their walk to develop your walk.

We must love God with all our heart, all our mind, all our strength, and all our very soul. God allows us to think whatever we want to think. The reward for thinking the way we want and doing it our way will result in an eternity of misery. God has set the criteria for entry into His presence for eternity. He desires for each of us, everyone, to be with Him. But we must trust and obey. My way will not work, only His way.

Look at me. Look at the problems I have caused myself by habitually saying no! What if I had started writing this book six years ago? God knew it would take six years of growth and six years of discipline for me to stop doing it my way. Each of us need to be in God's Word, searching for Him, proving what is good and what is not. We need to know, not think, in relation to God's will. Read the Bible. Study the Bible. Again, I suggest always praying first. Bring God right into the middle of what you are doing. Ask Him to open your mind and heart to what He has for you. I can tell you of people who read the Bible and still do not have a clue. It is not a fiction book you use to burn time. Do not speed read! Know what you are reading. Read to gain understanding of God. *Pray.* It will not be long and you will be reading the Bible for enjoyment. Once you start recognizing that God is making you aware of Him and He is growing you up to be who He wants you to be, you will not be able to get enough.

You cannot read the Bible like you are reading a novel and come to the understanding of God you need. We have to pray (talk to God) and we have to read His Word (listen to God). This is a conversation. You cannot have a conversation without two or more parties involved. God gets tired of people talking at Him. In fact, He says He does not listen. He wants people talking with Him. Read His Word—allow God to talk to you.

What should the church of God look like? God gives us a real good look at His church as recorded in the book of Acts. We know they all joined together constantly in prayer (Acts 1:14). We know they talked about Jesus openly (Acts 2). As recorded in Acts 2:22–23, Peter spoke openly, directly, frankly, bravely, and factually. Peter said, "Men of Israel listen to this: Jesus of Nazareth was a man accredited by God to you by miracles, wonders and signs, which God did among you through Him, as you yourselves know. This man was handed over to you by God's set purpose and foreknowledge; and you, with the help of wicked men, put Him to death by nailing Him to the cross." We know this type of speaking brought heartbreak which led to repentance (Acts 2:37 and 38).

Many were accepting the message, and thousands were being added to their number (Acts 2:41 and 47). We know the church members shared as there was need. We know from Acts 5 that many miraculous signs and wonders were accomplished among the people. Many were healed of various ailments. We know that day after day, in the temple courts and from house to house, they never stopped teaching and proclaiming the good news that Jesus is the Christ.

Using my church as an illustration, we have nine pastors on staff. Nine ordained ministers doing a variety of things. Our senior pastor does 90 percent of the preaching. They go home at four thirty or five if they even come to church at all. Does this imitate the model for us to follow in 2 Thessalonians 3:8–9? I would like to tell you they are in the "courts and going house to house," never stopping to preach and teach the good news. As the senior pastor's wife said, "They are working from home." God gives us the life of Jesus to imitate, and so we can have more specific illustrations, He gives us the life of Paul as a model to follow. As defined by God in His Word, Jesus and Paul's lives were dedicated to God in service to others.

David Scott, associate pastor, has not been to the food pantry in ten years—not for prayer, not to help with the labor, and not for encouragement. He works the food pantry from home. God calls us as teachers and preachers to set the example of service, and we do, good or bad. God says He will judge us more strictly. How can you describe the actions of my pastors? Worldly? 1 Corinthians 7:33 reads, "But a married man is concerned about the affairs of this world—how he can please his wife." This is not undivided devotion to the Lord.

Making the golf match, relaxing on your sailboat, being at a baseball game, making all the basketball practices, helping with homework, being available for every need at home, watching *Raymond* reruns, playing games with friends, or scheming with others in making new rules to improve the disciples of your flock are not evident in Jesus or Paul's model for us. Some of these things we should be involved in at times but they should not be our first love. When we ignore the needs of others, we ignore God. God says, "What you have done to the least of these you have done to me." If we are Christians, we are co-heirs with Christ. We have the responsibility to do God's will, not our will.

The leaders in the first-century Church said, "It would not be right for us to neglect the ministry of the Word of God in order to wait on tables." They said they wanted to give their attention to prayer and the ministry of the Word (Acts 6). At Chapel of the Flock Christian Church, our ministers will not attend prayer meetings on Wednesday nights. Two percent of the congregation attends on the Wednesdays Francis Raleigh facilitates. Less than 5 percent of the staff and elders attend on the Wednesdays Francis facilitates. In the other three Wednesday night prayer services which I facilitate, none of the staff and elders attend and .5 percent of the congregation attend. Can you see any reason in the world why God would not confirm His message in today's church?

I told you before that our senior pastor has been to six or seven Wednesday night prayer services that I facilitate in over four years. One other pastor came twice in four years. One elder came once in four years. I bring this up again because the pastor who came twice with his wife said to me after their second meeting, "Pete, what you guys are doing here on Wednesday nights is a good thing." Then he said, "But, Pete, this setting is a little too intimate for most people." Quite evidently he is right. The numbers show that he is right. A group of brothers and sisters sitting around talking to their Father, in His presence, is too intimate for most people. Why do these "most people" believe God will have them in His presence, intimately, for eternity, when they do not want to be in His presence intimately here?

The leaders of the first-century church devoted themselves to prayer and to the ministry of the Word of God, as previously noted. Our pastors today would rather wait tables. That is, they want to direct the money and delegate the work load. They want the flock to be "more responsible" disciples. Today's leaders want subordinates to be devoted to prayer and the ministry of the Word of God while they work from home.

I believe God is having me write this book because He has had about enough. I believe He sees that the very elect are about to be deceived! Jesus' return is near. This book is another Jonah giving warning to turn from our wide road to the narrow road that leads to the small gate. It is a shame that I can honestly make this statement. But using God's Word and the guilt we share when we condone each other's sin (Ezekiel 3:18–21, 33:4–6, Leviticus 19:17b, 2 John 9–10), knowing what God says, I believe every pastor and every elder at Chapel of the Flock Christian Church would be left behind if Jesus returned today. Signed contracts to become members of the church, changing God's Word, teaching worldly principles as God's principles, and living worldly idle lives will not be validation stamps for entry into heaven.

We know the early church lived in the fear of the Lord. We know they were strengthened and encouraged by the Holy Spirit (Acts 9:31). As well, we know God was adding to their numbers. God was healing and releasing people who were under the power of the devil. Disciples were worshipping, fasting, and praying. We know God was confirming His message "by enabling them to do miraculous signs and wonders" (Acts 14:3). God says in Acts 14:22 that we must go through many hardships to enter the kingdom of God. When we integrated the church and the world, we stopped the cruel physical hardships. What did we do to the spiritual blessing that came with the hardships? Is God confirming His message in your local body? He is not and cannot in our local body. It is not His message. As I mentioned, I had a discussion with one of the associate pastors about God confirming His message. The associate pastor said that God only did that during the apostolic period. I cannot disagree with him. It does appear that way but this would then infer God has changed. But we know God does not change. We know that God confirmed His Word through the apostles as well as His other disciples. The conclusion can only be that the message has changed and/or the world and the church of God do not go together.

I repeat myself, do not be deceived. God repeats this phrase throughout the Old and the New Testaments. God tells us through Paul in Acts 20:29– 31, "I know that after I leave, savage wolves will come in among you and will not spare the flock."(I spoke of this earlier; Paul said he would preach the message of God.) "Even from your own number men will arise and distort the truth in order to draw away disciples after them. So be on your guard! Remember that for three years I never stopped warning each of you night and day with tears." God holds us accountable to keep the gospel of God pure.

The leaders of the early church worked night and day as a model for us to follow. God says in Philippians 4:9 to put into practice those things we learned, received, heard, or have seen in Paul's life. Paul goes on to write, "And the God of peace will be with you." Do you think this could be the answer as to why God does not confirm His message? Our leaders are almost the opposite of Paul, certainly not like him. If we put these attributes of Paul's into practice, the God of peace will be with us. Since we do not put them into practice, maybe God is not with us. That would certainly explain His not confirming His message. Remember, we are, with everything we do, either serving God or ourselves. When we serve God, He calls it righteousness. When we are not serving Him, He calls it wickedness (Malachi 3:18).

What then? Should I wait for my pastors to illustrate by their walk, by their actions, my path? Certainly not! Yes, I am to aid them in their walk. I am to remove whatever wood is in my eye and witness to them in love. My eternal destination depends on my obedience, my love for God in action as my thanks to Him who did all the work. My eternity is my responsibility. I am also responsible for those who look to me for Christian leadership. This is my responsibility as co-heir with Christ.

The first-century church preached God's message, and the listeners were cut to the heart. We talked earlier about Acts 2:23 "This man (Jesus) was *handed over to you* by God's set purpose and foreknowledge, and *you*, with the help of wicked men, put Him to death by nailing Him to the cross." I did not hear him say this but the media widely claimed that the pope said the people of Israel were not guilty for Jesus' death. This may be politically correct, but God says in Acts 2:22 "Men of Israel" and in Acts 2:23 "handed over to you"—"and you, with the help of wicked men, put Him to death." I do not consider it smart to call God a liar. Stop! The pope and I are just as guilty as the men of Israel.

Should we not be thanking the men of Israel? If they had not put Jesus to death, you and I would have no hope for eternity with God.

Remember, this was God's set purpose. Jesus could have stopped the entire happening. He had the power. All Jesus had to do was ask His Father, and His Father would have put more than twelve legions of angels at Jesus' disposal (Matthew 26:53). This is our illustration of meekness. Jesus had within His control the ability to stop this living hell but was obedient to His Father, meek and obedient, for you and me.

Jesus' obedience provided a bridge past our sins to God. And because of His sacrifice, we have the right to become children of God. Jeremiah the prophet told of this centuries before when he said those circumcised in the flesh only would be punished. We all must be circumcised of the heart by Jesus. Those of us that are circumcised of the heart by Jesus are Jews.

The people of Israel are the chosen people—that is, the people to whom God chose to reveal Himself to the world. Theirs is the adoption as sons not by the written code, but through the promise of God, not by natural birth but through rebirth. The natural branches refused to believe so because of unbelief; the natural branches were broken off, and because of our faith, we have been grafted in. We should not take this matter lightly or arrogantly. We should consider the situation for what it is and be forever thankful and obedient.

Those of us who call ourselves Christlike or Christians should look the part. That is, we should be obedient to God the Father and should serve others even before ourselves. Serving God and serving others is really the same discipline. We show our love for God in how we serve others. Jesus explains this better than I ever could in Matthew 25: 31–46.

"When the Son of Man comes in His glory, and all the angels with Him, He will sit on His throne in heavenly glory. All the nations will be gathered before Him, and He will separate the people one from another as a shepherd separates the sheep from the goats. He will put the sheep on His right and the goats on His left. Then the King will say to those on His right, 'Come, you who are blessed by my Father; take your inheritance, the kingdom prepared for you since the creation of the world. For I was hungry and you gave me something to eat, I was thirsty and you gave me something to drink, I was a stranger and you invited me in, I needed clothes and you clothed me, I was sick and you looked after me, I was in prison and you came to visit me.' Then the righteous will answer Him, 'Lord, when did we see you hungry and feed you, or thirsty and give you something to drink? When did we see you a stranger and invite you in or needing clothes and clothe you? When did we see you sick or in prison and go to visit you?' The King will reply, 'I tell you the truth, whatever you did for one of the least of these brothers of mine, you did for me.' Then He will say to those on His left, depart from me, you who are accursed, into the eternal fire prepared for the devil and his angels. For I was hungry and you gave me nothing to eat; I was thirsty and you gave me nothing to drink, I was a stranger and you did not invite me in, I needed clothes and you did not clothe me, I was sick and in prison and you did not look after me.' They will also answer, 'Lord, when did we see you hungry or thirsty or a stranger or needing clothes or sick or in prison, and did not help you?' He will reply, 'I tell you the truth, whatever you did not do for one of the least of these, you did not do for me.' Then they will go away to eternal punishment, but the righteous to eternal life."

We justify ourselves in what we do and do not do by comparing ourselves to the rest of the world. We do not compare ourselves to Jesus. If we did, we would stop doing what we are doing and we would start doing what we are not doing. We need to remove ourselves from our worldly ways and our worldly thinking.

The early church did not have a Participating Member's class complete with signed contracts that were mandatory before acceptance. As Jesus pointed out, what you have done to the least of these you have done to Him. Leaders who demand an individual take a mandatory class and sign a contract are putting the same restrictions on the Son of God.

The leaders of the early church worked night and day and preached the gospel message for free. Not because they did not have a right to the financial help, but as a model for us to follow so as not to hinder the gospel. Our leaders do not want to do what we pay them for, let alone anything beyond their job description. The leaders of today's churches are the Pharisees and Sadducees of the twenty-first century.

We, the preachers and teachers, are crucifying Jesus again and again when we add or subtract anything from God's Word. Every time we teach something the way we want it and not how God teaches it, we are in rebellion. At that point, we are a member of the devil's army and not God's. God says we cannot serve two masters. When we say God has first place in our lives, but our lives clearly indicate that God is important but not first and most important, we establish a lie to be truth. That is, when congregants see that our wives, sons, daughters, parents, and free time are most important, the lie becomes truth. Congregants see that "God has first place in my life" statement actually means He has a subordinate position but that is the way it should be. This is what James Cantrell and Francis Raleigh teach and therefore they create disciples who fall short of God's rest.

I use the thinking of James and Francis concerning their love and devotion to their wives, sons, daughters, and parents and how they teach their devotion to them in relation to God. This teaching is not consistent with God's Word. We all do have the obligation to be good husbands, fathers, and sons, but this obligation is second to our obligation to be totally devoted to God. And certainly the apostles who left everything to follow Jesus did not sin. God Himself did not sin when He gave His Son as a ransom for us all. In fact, Francis, two months and two days after preaching the message that pastors who spent more time with the members of their congregation and with people in the community were sinning in that effort, stating they should be more devoted to their wives and children, delivered a message on love, what love is. Francis used 1 John 3:16, which reads, "This is how we know what love is: Jesus Christ laid down His life for us. And we

ought to lay down our lives for our brothers." Francis also used 1 John
4:9-11, which reads, "This is how God showed His love among us: He
sent His one and only Son into the world that we might live through
Him. This is love: not that we loved God, but that He loved us and sent
His Son as an atoning sacrifice for our sins. Dear friends, since God so
loved us, we also ought to love one another."

Francis did a really fine job with this message. Francis and I conversed
about the message on August 21, 2011, where he said pastors were
committing a sin in their dedication to the Lord. To put it mildly, he
and I do not agree. As Francis delivered this message two months
later, which is the exact opposite message, he looked at me throughout
the sermon and I knew that he knew he was delivering two different
messages.

The leaders of the church during Jesus' life protected their position in
life above all else—even if one man should die to protect his way of
life in this world. Do the leaders during Jesus' life sound quite similar
to the leaders of today?

I wrote a letter to our senior pastor, Francis Raleigh, and I sent a copy
to the chairman of the board of elders. The chairman is ultimately
responsible for all the church. I outlined my concerns with so often
misrepresenting God's Word. I have given you but a few instances;
there are many more. One topic I wrote about is tithing. As I said
before, our doctrinal stance is 10 percent of gross income before taxes.
Francis and I have had a conversation about tithing. Francis told me he
had studied tithing and it really should be 26 percent annually.

I hope you read God's Word and test everything. As I read God's
Word, one of the many things that stands out is that God wants to
be in a relationship with each of us. The Old and New Testaments
tell of God's desire for us to come to an understanding of who He
is. In this life, we will never fully understand. But God desires us to
seek Him. God wants to be found by each of us. When we come to an
understanding of God, we will be in awe. We will revere Him. God

wants us to understand Him because He knows when we do, we will revere Him. All the sacrifices that God required were designed to bring us into God's presence. This is true about the annual tithe as well. I talked about tithe before, but I want to spend a little more time on it. I am hoping to give you enough information that you will want to prove me right or wrong.

God tells us very clearly in Deuteronomy that He wants to spend time with us by His design and within the parameters He has set. The tithe in the first and second years was to be eaten in His presence by each of us at a location chosen by God. God wants us to spend time with Him and learn to revere Him (Deuteronomy 14:23). When we read scripture knowing this is God's design and desire, the others passages on tithing become much more clear. With God's Word so clear on the subject, why is it taught so differently? I have some statements and positions by other teachers that I would like to share with you to help answer that question.

I have been in the church nearly thirty years under four different senior pastors and many associate pastors. Never has anyone taught what God spells out in Deuteronomy as to tithing. I truly believe there is only one truth. All else is a lie. People from many different churches are questioning the 10 percent of gross income before taxes as a must. It is always taught as a must. If you do not tithe 10 percent every year, you are robbing God. People are reading the Bible more and more thoroughly. People realize when God says, "Each man should give what he has decided in his heart to give, not reluctantly or under compulsion, for God loves a cheerful giver," there is no set amount or portion. The Holy Spirit is real and is teaching those seeking truth.

I mentioned that today's leaders are the Pharisees and Sadducees of the twenty-first century. They are trying to protect their position just like those Pharisees of the first century. Are you able to read the writing on the wall? As the Holy Spirit teaches those seeking the truth, people are going to demand their leaders model Paul's life. I cannot imagine David Scott working, let alone working day and night.

As I said, disputes are arising all over the world concerning tithing. Congregants are disputing leadership claims concerning giving. The backlash of this dispute over giving extends far beyond money. Congregants do not trust their leadership. When our leaders continually exploit funds for church needs, it causes not only distrust but also liberal attitudes about anything leadership teaches. When congregants realize their leaders are teaching falsely about one thing, individuals find it hard to believe anything.

Many churches are using a wide variety of methods to obtain funds from individuals. Some churches have automated deductions from accounts. Some have set up debit card and credit card kiosks within the church building. The Reverend Marty Baker, pastor at Stevens Creek Church in Augusta, Georgia, created a giving kiosk machine that allows congregants to donate to the church from their bank cards. Reverend Baker and his wife created SecureGive, a for-profit company, which has many different kiosks in many different churches. These kiosks also help in the tracking of who is giving their fair share.

In Gainesville, Georgia, Crown Financial Ministries offers courses to teach churchgoers how to save, budget, and get out of debt, yet still give 10 percent of their income to their church. The Reverend Ralph Peters (no relation) began offering Crown classes at his church a few years ago. He says giving went up 30 percent the very first year. Churches will teach the dictates of the classes, which include voiding yourself of credit cards and, at the same time, offer kiosk machines so you can use bank cards to give.

Many individuals have spoken up about the teaching of adhering to the law in regards to tithing. As in my case, I spoke up personally and in writing. I got no response at all. Some congregants have been asked to leave their church. Some have received letters putting them in their place. One such individual received a letter quoting Hebrews 13:17, which reads, "Obey your leaders and submit to them, for they keep watch over your souls as those who will give account." The leaders, who wrote this letter to force a brother to shut up and obey, disregarded the part that says, "As those who will give account." Their judgment will be harsh. God says, "Test everything," and He says very often, "Do not be deceived." Most pastors teach the tithing law. They probably believe as does Francis Raleigh in the *except* clause. That is, the clause no one can find that says Jesus "cancelled the written code" with its regulations, He took it away, nailing it to the cross *except* for money matters.

We must take God's Word, the Bible, in its entirety. If you keep the law and stumble on just one point, you are guilty of breaking the whole law. God says if you adhere to one point of the law, you are obligated to do the whole law. And for those who desire to find justification in the law, Jesus the Christ will be of no value to you. You have fallen away from grace.

Many pastors use Hebrews 7 as a springboard to teach tithing. Hebrews 7:5 clearly states that tithing is required by law. Colossians 2:14 states the law was taken away; it was nailed to the cross. Pastors like to use Melchizedek as the sample along with Hebrews 7. Melchizedek was the king of Salem as well as a high priest. Abraham gave Melchizedek 10 percent of the spoils Abraham had recovered. Pastors like to use this as their basis for tithing since Jesus is called a high priest like Melchizedek. This line of thinking is totally without merit. First, Abraham was a very wealthy man in livestock and silver and gold (Genesis 13:2). The king of Sodom told Abraham to give him his people and keep the goods for himself (Genesis 14:21). Abraham refused anything (Genesis 14:23). Abraham was a righteous man. Abraham gave 90 percent of the spoils to the king of Sodom, asking only what his men had eaten and a fair share for his men (Genesis 14:24). Abraham gave zero of his own wealth, not 1 percent, not 10 percent —zero.

There are a lot of articles written that explore the thoughts and opinions on tithing. Most reveal the lack of faith from church leadership and the willingness of leadership to pervert the gospel for money. The love of money is a root of all kinds of evil. To recap tithing and Abraham, Abraham was a righteous man because he believed God. Abraham gave 10 percent of the war spoils to Melchizedek, king of Salem. Abraham kept zero of the war spoils for himself so no one could say, "I made Abram rich" (Genesis 14:23). Abraham was very wealthy. Abraham gave none of his possessions, assets, or income. Abraham gave 10 percent of something of which he wanted no part. This is hardly a justification for the *except* clause theory. Remember, the *except* clause theory is the unwritten law that states Jesus "cancelled the written code" *except* in the area of your money.

Reading the New Testament, especially the books Paul wrote, God tells us the love of money is not good. Why then do pastors love your money so much? I believe that question is best answered by God's Word. Paul tells us he will put up with anything in order not to hinder the gospel. He works day and night. He preaches God's message and works with his hands. Paul "stayed for a year and a half" with the Corinthians, teaching them the Word of God and working with them making tents (Acts 18). God says in Acts 20:34 that Paul's hands supplied the needs of himself and his companions. Paul asks the question, "Is it only I and Barnabas who must work for a living?" God says a worker is worthy of his wages. God is saying if you work, you have a right to be paid. But God gives us Paul as an example, as a model to follow. Paul says he does not use this right. He preaches for free. I believe the answer to the above question is the same answer as the answer to this question. Why do pastors not follow the model God gives us, Paul? Gold fever is a worldly trait. Having divided interest is a worldly trait. Friendship with the world makes you an enemy of God. Does this help explain why God does not confirm His message in today's church?

God measures our obedience to Him by what we do or do not do for others. We are to remove stumbling blocks, not add them. We are called to seek the good of others before we seek our own good. We preach and listen to the Word of God and ignore what God says. We, therefore, deceive ourselves by not practicing God's Word.

Deceit in America

We Americans love to deceive and we love to be deceived. For decades we have allowed our presidents, senators, and congressmen to use our tax dollars to pay companies to move out of the United States. Industry after industry has vacated the United States and we have paid them to do so. Now, the largest dollar industry in this country is all but gone, and that is the auto industry. We have 20 million people out of work and we wonder why. We are a smart nation, just ask us. We keep right on buying foreign-made whatever we want. We like to deceive and we like to deceive ourselves.

There is a movement among the people of the United States. It is currently being called the Occupy Wall Street Movement. People are extremely irritated in regards to their position in life. People are jobless, without money, and many are homeless. The people want satisfaction from those running the country. Yes, our leaders have led us astray as they have for four thousand years. God gave the best description possible when He called Samaria and Jerusalem prostitutes. What are the leaders of this country who have used the American people's money to become richer? What are they who have deceived the American people to elevate the rest of the world and drag down the people of this country? What are they who disregard our constitution and rape the people of the United States? What are they who murder a United States' president and cover it up as well as condone the murder? They are sons of their father, the father of lies.

People of America: the leadership is to blame but we are the accomplices. You do not have a job? Where was your car made? There is a well-known fact, widely published during the seventies and eighties, that said, "For every foreign-made automobile sold in the United States, ten Americans lose their job." Americans, Jesus said it correctly: you are either for me or you are against me. What is in your driveway? Jesus also said that every kingdom divided against itself will be ruined. We allow these people to deceive us. God says over and over, do not be deceived.

On November 22, 1963, we had a president murdered. Our government leaders spent millions of dollars investigating the murder. Over fourteen thousand FBI man-hours alone went into investigating the murder of John F. Kennedy. The findings the government gave us are totally impossible. We have accepted it for fifty years. There is a paper trail. There is a clear picture. There is a major motive. But no one really wants to know. I mean, if they can kill a president, if they can change the money, if they skirt the constitution, why get hurt? The answer is heaven or hell. Be silent and hope God does not hold our silence against us or shake Satan's assembly of prostitutes.

Our Constitution is supposed to be our supreme law, our foundation for all law. Do you ever read the Constitution of the United States of America? Take the time to read Article 1, Section 10 of the Constitution. We do not teach this anymore in this country, but the reason Article 1, Section 10 was put in the Constitution was so we would never have paper money again. The Continental Congress issued continental currency to finance the war. When they needed more money, they printed it. Sound familiar? Inflation got so bad in the late 1770s that $100 would not buy a pound of potatoes. In 1780, Congress redeemed about $125 million of continental currency at two cents for each dollar. The rest was not redeemed. Therefore, the saying "not worth a continental" came into being.

The government leaders told us we could not have gold and silver as legal tender. Carrying coins would cost too much because of wear and reproduction costs. Why did Congress in 2005 make a law establishing one dollar coins? The non-partisan Government Accountability Office reported switching from paper to metal would save $5.5 billion over thirty years. We are currently storing $1.2 billion in one dollar coins at a cost, and we are making more. Continually God tells us, "Do not be deceived."

Ten days before JFK was murdered, he gave a speech at Columbia University in which he stated, "The high office of president has been used to foment a plot to destroy the Americans' freedom, and before I leave office I must inform the citizen of his plight." Forty years ago this speech was easily found; today, try to find it. One fact I know is that every Federal Reserve note prior to 1963 said on the note, "This note is legal tender for all debts public and private and is redeemable in *lawful* money at the United States Treasury or at any Federal Reserve Bank."

After 1963, Federal Reserve notes said, "This note is legal tender for all debts public and private." Only gold certificates, silver certificates, and United States notes said, "This note is legal tender for all debts public and private" before 1963. In 1963 the JFK Administration started printing United States notes again. United States notes can be easily recognized. The serial numbers are red. The fact is that all Federal Reserve notes were "redeemable in lawful money" and then one president dies and now they *are* lawful money.

When money is loaned into the banking system, the party initially loaning the money receives the interest on that money. If United States notes are loaned into the system by the United States Treasury, the United States of America raises money through that system. If Federal Reserve notes are loaned into the banking system, the Federal Reserve receives all revenue. The Federal Reserve Banking System is an independent company, separate from the United States government. All interest money for originating the money goes to the Federal Reserve system.

If the United States Treasury used only United States notes, you and I would not be paying income taxes. The Federal Reserve has raped the American people of trillions of dollars, and yes, the leaders of this country are prostitutes. Benedict Arnold is a national hero compared to the individuals who have held federal offices over the last fifty years.

We are deceived by our church leaders. We are deceived by our government leaders. We deceive ourselves with what we buy. If you spend $2.00 on a pair of foreign-made socks, what have you hurt? If you spend $200 - $300 on yourself in a lifetime, how badly are you hurting your country, your neighbor? However, when you spend $40,000 on a foreign-made car every other year, $2 million over a fifty-year adult life, how badly have you hurt your country, your neighbor? Just take a look; you are there.

Unfortunately churches follow trends too. Many of the mega churches are coming to the realization that staying away from hardcore Biblical teaching, which has worked for the last twenty-five to thirty years, is no longer growing attendance. The Baby Boomer era of "leave me alone and let me do my thing" will not work to enlarge your church. I believe there are two main reasons. People are reading their Bibles and thus seeking truth. As well, I believe Jesus' return is very near. The bottom line is that the Holy Spirit of God is active in a mighty way, with or without our help. People want authenticity, not a show or lip service. People are looking for those doing the walk. People recognize those who have faith but no works; death is very recognizable.

God has been speaking to us continually all along. Some people are starting to listen. And therefore it is becoming much more difficult to talk the talk and not walk the walk. But again, most people are blind to what is happening around them. Very few are in the Bible daily, testing everything. I will continue to repeat myself on the subject of God's Word. Pray and ask God to lead you in your reading. Sincerely seek God; you will be amazed how He reveals things to you. Test everything!

Why do we wait for schemes and stratagems from our leaders? The change must start with the person in the mirror. We must demand truth in everything. But we must be able to recognize truth and we must be able to recognize lies. Anything outside the whole truth is a lie. Our eternal destination is in the balance. Each of us will appear before the judgment seat of Christ. Our lives will dictate where we spend eternity. Not that we can earn it, because we cannot earn eternity with God. But we must accept the gift and our lives must say, "Thank you, Jesus."

Living a life that says, "Thank you," is living a life of service to others, imitating Jesus. The only life that pleases God and is victorious is Jesus' life. We have to put to death our desires of the flesh daily, actually moment by moment. We cannot allow our self-centeredness to deter us from eternity with our sovereign creator. We must put into practice the disciplines of obedience to God.

I was talking with a dear sister last week. She was concerned with our leadership at Chapel of the Flock Christian Church. Specifically, she was talking about pastors and elders not setting the proper example for the congregation. She hated to speak of it because she felt like she lacked leadership skills. She was once an employee of Kingsland Community Church and she spent years recovering from that experience. I know her well and her desire to serve God. She does a lot of things. Her heart is wonderful. She desires to be the daughter that God wants her to be. She feels insignificant in her self-appraised skill set. I told her during that conversation, "I truly believe you are one of the greatest leaders in this church." I told her that because it is true. She feels she doesn't have anything to offer and what little she does have is insignificant. She works a job forty to sixty hours a week. She and her husband are at every Wednesday night prayer service. They are at church and Sunday school every week. They attend a Tuesday night Bible study. I told her, "Bev, you and Mike, along with another couple, are at church forty minutes early every Sunday to pray pew by pew for every person in each service." This is service. The greatest leader to ever walk this earth was Jesus. Jesus served by example. I said to her, "Can you imagine what would happen if the twelve hundred other individuals who attend here each Sunday were equal in service to you and Mike? Can you, Bev, imagine what would happen if our nine ministers on staff spent as much time in service above their jobs as you do?" I answered my own question. I said emphatically that God would move miraculously among us.

The impact each of us has on others and outside the church is immense, both positively and negatively. We are the windows through which

Jesus is seen. Others are watching and grading our walk, especially those in leadership positions.

There is a man close to me. I have been praying for him and witnessing to him for years. He knows he is a good guy. He sees himself in comparison to those around him. He is a good person but somewhat self-centered. He is a giving person. If he likes you, he will go to about any limit for you. He has worked all his life, as most of us have. He feels sorry for the jobless and poor but keeps himself at a distance. This distancing, I think, is a "protect his heart" philosophy. He does not attend church. He lives next door to a preacher. By the fruit he knows, he is ten times the Christian as the pastor next door. He helps his neighbors often. He does not read the Bible. He does not know God but he does know of Him.

I was talking with him about two years ago, cautiously, as I must. I was sharing with him some of the things going on in my family and he was sharing some of the things going on in his. I started talking about Chapel of the Flock Christian Church. I mentioned that Francis Raleigh was going to start having Wednesday night prayer service on the fourth Wednesday of each month in the worship center. He immediately responded, "Sure, he should be happy to start doing 25 percent of what he should have been doing all along." My friend knew I had been facilitating the Wednesday night meeting for over two years. I did not respond. I started talking about something entirely different. I had lost my positive witness. My friend lives next door to a pastor. He knows what they do and do not do. And, he was right. Someone on staff should be setting a good example instead of a poor one. My friend is a guy outside the church and he sees and knows what is and is not going on. How will we win him to Jesus?

Conclusion

There are churches with great success stories. Some have attendance of thirty thousand to forty thousand each Sunday. These numbers are wonderful. If the message is truly God's message, the numbers are wonderful. If the message is anything less or more, it is a lie and the developing disciples are on the wrong team. Many of these huge (in numbers) churches teach that God wants us to be rich. That is, they teach that God wants us to be financially rich and that sounds good to us. So we jump on that train of thought. We see the benefit of having a great life here on earth and eternity in heaven. Remember, God says, "Anyone who chooses to be a friend of the world becomes an enemy of God" (James 4:4). God also says through Jesus in Luke 12:15, "Watch out! Be on your guard against all kinds of greed; a man's life does not consist in the abundance of his possessions." God also says how hard it is for the rich to enter the kingdom of God (Mark 10:23). Again in Mark 10:24, He says, "Children, how hard it is to enter the kingdom of God!"

The kingdom of God is a free gift, but it is hard to enter it. Why? Because of self-centeredness, selfishness, and the lack of desire to be like Jesus, a servant. God wants us to have a more abundant life. Do you think He means what He says through Jude, Jesus' brother? Jude 2 says mercy, peace and love be yours in abundance. Test everything!

The rich young man Jesus talks about in Matthew 19 had kept all the commandments. The young man's question was, "What good thing must I do to get eternal life?" Look at the question: *thing* is singular. Jesus tells him, "If you want to be perfect, go sell your possessions and give them to the poor, and you will have treasure in heaven. Then come, follow me." God tells us, where your treasure is, there your heart will be also. Jesus did not say give your wealth to the church, nor did He say give it to the leaders. Jesus said if you want to be "perfect," give to the poor. God wants what is best for us. This is eternal language. Those who have ears, let them hear.

We have a smorgasbord of churches and beliefs from which we can choose. We can believe anything we want. If we cannot find exactly what we want to believe, we can just start a new way, as did Joseph Smith. And in our social correctness, we will call it Christianity. This is what we have in this world today. This works out great here on this earth because we are on friendly terms with the prince of this world, who is the devil. God promises us we will have hell as payment for our adultery. Each of us is obligated to prove or disprove what is taught in our churches. If the teaching is not 100 percent correct, we must speak up or share in their guilt.

To imitate Jesus is to serve others, to obey God and to delight in the fear of the Lord our God. Jesus showed anger when the house of God was used improperly. We should show the same concern if we are imitating Him. Do you think God has this illustration in His Word for a purpose?

I have given you a description of the leadership in the church that I have and am dealing with. I know your experiences are similar. Lack of enthusiasm from leadership and congregants is unfortunately world-wide. Today's church, as we know and accept it, is entangled with the world. Individually and collectively, we have a very difficult time being in the world and not of the world. He who masquerades as an angel of light has been very successful in his deception. God has given us fair warning. He has written it down and kept the information available to us for more than twenty centuries. Those of us who preach and teach and say that God has first place in our lives while our lives clearly show that God does not have our undivided devotion are without an excuse. We sin and we cause others to sin because we have taught these little ones who believe in Him to imitate our divided devotion (1 Corinthians 7:33–35). God must sit on the throne of our lives 100 percent of the time. Not from eight to five and then we are off the clock. God is extremely serious when He gives us Paul to imitate, and then God says that Paul works with his hands. Paul works day and night. Paul preaches the gospel for free. Paul does this not because he does not have a right to be paid for his preaching labor. Paul does this as a model for us to follow.

I know most people do not understand total devotion. I do not know why, except the world's influence is so great. God expects total undivided devotion. God knows He deserves it because of who He is. I do not believe we will ever have a satisfactory understanding of God until we can grasp total undivided devotion. First of all, you will probably never get there—especially if you are married and have children. I believe we all need this understanding of the awesome, wonderful God we are to serve.

I want to give you some things to read. I ask that you pray and ask God to grant you the understanding He wants you to have. Then read Matthew 19. The discussion is about divorce. Jesus takes the conversation to verse 12, where Jesus states some have renounced marriage because of the kingdom of heaven. The one who can accept this should accept it. I want God to explain this to you. Read 1 Corinthians 7:1 "It is good for a man not to marry." Look at verses 6 and 7. God wants all men to be like Paul—single but "as a concession" he allows marriage because of "immorality" (verse 2). In 1 Corinthians 7:32–35, God gives us direction on undivided devotion. He tells us if you are married you are concerned about the affairs of this world. God gives us another picture of undivided devotion in Revelation 14:4: "These are those who did not defile themselves with women, for they kept themselves pure. They follow the Lamb wherever He goes." I hope God will give you the eyes to see.

Yes, God gave Eve to Adam as a "suitable helper" (Genesis 2:20). Satan deceived the woman (Genesis 3:13). God created dry ground and saw that it was good (Genesis 1:9–10). Because Adam listened to his wife, God cursed the ground that He saw was good (Genesis 3:17). Sin changed everything forever. Where was Adam's devotion? Where is Jesus' devotion? (Matthew 26:39).

Each of us, through understanding, must put everything in its proper position. We who are teachers and preachers will be judged more strictly. As preachers and teachers, we are to be examples of following the model described to us so clearly by God. No deviations are acceptable. We cannot pick and choose the disciplines we will and will not adhere to, especially as leaders. We must not invent stumbling blocks to lighten our load or maintain our idle time. Our modern organizational theory taught to us to measure and control disciples is complete ignorance on our part. If we as leaders practice God's simple disciplines and teach them, God will do the rest. We have His word on that. Currently we are too smart to do it God's way. We have been taught to plan, scheme, manipulate, and even lie to generate disciples. The problem is that we are generating disciples just like us. Let us stop being so smart and allow the Holy Spirit of God to have full control and authority to teach and lead.

Our churches have become impotent religious institutions that are living examples of James 2:26: "Faith without works is dead." If you attend church every Sunday, you have done very little for God. Let us say you attend church every Sunday. You attend a Sunday school class as well. You meet once a week for a Bible study with a small group. These things are good, but what have you done for God? You are learning and hopefully growing in your relationship with God but you are not doing anything for God unless you are putting into practice the things you are learning each moment of each day. We must be gathering with Jesus or we are scattering.

Let me give you a hypothetical situation using myself as the teacher. I teach a class three days a week on running a marathon. I teach breathing techniques, racing strategies, and what to look for and expect during the race. The class meets for four weeks with eleven days of instruction and discussion. On the last day, we have a final exam and that's it. You never run a marathon. You never run a race. You never put into practice what you have learned. What have you accomplished? If you learn but do not practice what you learn, you are hurting God, not helping Him.

There are many people attending church but few are practicing the principals God has set for serving one another. Not practicing these principals is disobedience. This again is what Jesus is talking about in Matthew 7:13–14. The *highway* to heaven leads to destruction and the *narrow road* leads to life. God's church can be found inside the factitious churches that are everywhere. The members of God's church have visible fruit. God has first place in their lives. They do not need to tell you. You can see the difference. In fact, when you use the F word all week long, you are scattering, not gathering. The F word, whether used with a U or an R, means the same thing and is unacceptable. This is cursing and is inappropriate in any setting.

There are a number of persons who want to be in God's will. It is extremely difficult for them to shake the confusion by which they are guided. Only by God's grace will we be successful. As I have said before, the only life that pleases the Father is the Son's. For this reason, these days will be cut short, for the sake of the elect. God foretold in His Word twenty centuries ago that we would be in this situation. He knew that we would fall to this point. We have allowed all that He said would happen to happen. *We* are no different today than they were two thousand years ago or thirty-five hundred years ago.

God allowed the pharaohs of Egypt great successes. As their success stories grew so did their pride and arrogance. God allowed the pharaohs to get to a point in their self-edification for His own glorification. God told beforehand that that would happen; it did and has throughout the history of man. Yet we still do not believe.

Look at me. I used simple saving disciplines and God allowed me to have my dreams. But because of my disobedience in writing this book and/or because God did not have His proper place in my life, forty-plus years of savings were wiped out. For our eternal sake, God cannot allow for us to be successful without Him in His proper place.

We cannot have the proper relationship with God by just going through the motions—not the relationship God wants. We must make prayer foundational in everything we do. God wants to be involved in everything we do, great and small. There are no limits on what God will do through our lives if our lives are His. The possibilities are beyond our imaginations.

Jesus spent a lot of time in prayer, so much so that His disciples asked Him to teach them to pray. Jesus stayed connected to God in prayer, just like recharging a battery. We should spend a lot of time in prayer as well if we want to be fully charged. The most efficient way out of the stands as a spectator of God's message is to participate in His message through prayer. Did you know by not praying for someone, you are sinning against God (1 Samuel 12:23)?

Jesus was totally devoted to God, His Father, and to His Father's will. As an illustration of how we are today compared to Jesus, our benchmark: Francis Raleigh cancelled the Wednesday night prayer session on the fourth Wednesday of November 2011 because it was before the four-day weekend of Thanksgiving. We do not want to be inconvenienced by God! Francis moved the service he facilitates to the fifth Wednesday night of November. The normal Wednesday night prayer could not get in the church on the fourth Wednesday night because the church was locked.

When we met on the fifth Wednesday night of November 2011, not one of our nine pastors was in attendance. Francis Raleigh did not attend. He had a prior engagement. Not one of our twelve elders was able to attend either. We had eighteen people in attendance out of a congregation of twelve hundred. December 25, 2011, Christmas Day, we were pleasantly surprised to see in our church bulletin that the Wednesday night prayer service was scheduled for December 28 in the worship center. Francis Raleigh had not cancelled the last Wednesday night prayer service of the year as he had in December 2010. However, when we arrived on December 28, there were no vehicles in the parking lot. My wife and I were able to enter the church but found out later it was because they were expecting a cable TV service representative. Seven people showed up for the prayer service, but no pastor or elder were available. What we thought was going to be an hour of prayer with our senior pastor in the worship center ended up being an hour of prayer with brothers and sisters in Christ in the vestibule. The year 2011 ended with God having the same "first place" He had all year. Our leadership was AWOL.

I was prayerfully hoping 2012 would be different. I had hoped Francis Raleigh would vacate the misuse of scripture after so many years of prompting, especially after the last several months of intense dialogue, both verbal and written. Francis spent four weeks of January 2012 preaching on giving. He had just preached on giving a few weeks earlier, October 30, 2011. I had a couple visiting that week. They had visited a few months earlier, and Francis was preaching on giving then as well. This sticks out to me because after two visits, Katie said she would never be back.

During the four weeks of messages on giving and being generous in January 2012, Francis referred to 1 Corinthians 16:2, 2 Corinthians 8:3, and 2 Corinthians 9:6–11. He preached giving should be every week, on Sunday, 10 percent of your gross pay, systematic and regular. Francis taught this as God's instructions from 1 Corinthians 16:2. He taught giving should be sacrificial as illustrated in 2 Corinthians 8:3. Francis said that he was not a legalist, but the chosen people of Israel gave 23 percent. If you remember, in the conversation he and I had on the truth of tithing, he told me 26 percent. The point is, in four weeks of preaching from these scriptures on giving, he never mentioned that Paul stayed the winter in Corinth and no collections were made while he was there (1 Corinthians 16:2, 5–7 and Acts 19:21–22). Francis also never mentioned that the foundation for his teaching was a one-time gift for the saints in Jerusalem, which was a year in coming. Please refer to 1 Corinthians 16:1; 2 Corinthians 8:10, 20; and 2 Corinthians 9:1–2.

I knew the message for February 5, 2012, was going to be from 2 John. I know what God says throughout His Word from Deuteronomy 4:2 to Revelation 22:18–19, "Do not add to or subtract from His Word." As a

Sunday school teacher, I could not share that our pastors are habitually not truthful. Because 2 John 11 (NAS) says, "For the one who gives him a greeting participates in his evil deeds," I felt led to resign as Sunday school teacher after class on January 29, 2012.

Pastors and teachers of God's message, as well as elders, are representatives of God. Our illustration, our walk, is either good or bad. We are either gathering or scattering. There is no middle ground. The members of Chapel of the Flock Christian Church are a mirror image of its leadership—complacent, not anywhere close to Jesus' illustration in the garden.

Each of our pastors and elders openly state that God has first place in their lives. God has a place in their lives, but not first place. A four-day weekend for Thanksgiving is more important. Anything is more important on Wednesday night than meeting with God and His children for prayer.

Pray about whatever is on your mind. Jesus prayed three different times in the garden before His arrest. He asked God if it be possible for Him not to have to do what he was about to do—may it pass from Him. Jesus was about to let sinful men harm Him beyond recognition. Jesus did not want to do His will as much as He wanted to do His Father's will. This is where we need to be! This is where we fail God so miserably.

We say we love God. We say God has first place in our lives. Brothers and sisters in Christ and those outside the family of God look at our lives as leaders and can *plainly* see that we put our spouses, our children, our parents, our free time, and other things ahead of God. Therefore, this manner of thought seems permissible. Pastors such as Francis Raleigh preach it is a sin to spend so much of your time with others such as your congregation and community and not be devoted to your family. We accept this as the way it should be because it serves our selfishness. We do not recognize that God deserves *all* our hearts, *all* our minds, *all* our souls, and *all* our strengths.

Corruption

I was not at Columbia University on November 12, 1963. I got that quote from a book written forty years ago. I know JFK was murdered, and our government explanation is not accurate. I know what the constitution says, and we do not follow it. I know the Federal Reserve money prior to 1963 was redeemable in lawful money. I know after 1963, Federal Reserve money became legal tender. I do not know why all money loaned into the banking system, the originating interest, does not belong to the people of the United States of America, who make the money secure. I believe the people involved in the murder of JFK will have hell as a reward. I also believe all who condone the cover-up, the deception, and the cost to the people of the United States are just as guilty. I believe they are guilty of more than just murder, whether congressmen, senators, or presidents.

The marriage between the Church of God and Rome (the world) speaks for itself. Look at the last two thousand years, as far as what the church was, is, and has been. There is a reason when the Apostle John saw the woman he was "greatly astonished" (Revelation 17:6). In Revelation 17:9, God tells us through John, "This calls for a mind with wisdom. The seven heads are seven hills on which the woman sits." Revelation 17:18 says, "The woman you saw is the great city that rules over the kings of the earth. Anyone who chooses to be a friend of the world becomes an enemy of God."

The Occupy Wall Street Movement, which is spreading rapidly and with good reason, is a result of all this deception. The individuals who are and have been in office are at fault. But the root cause is evil. Like it or not, that is the way it is. We as Americans can do what we want. We have the freedom to do so. However, the exercise of this freedom can be harmful. God says it this way in 1 Corinthians 6:12: "Everything is permissible for me but not everything is beneficial. Everything is permissible for me but I will not be mastered by anything." Exercising our freedom to buy foreign-made products, especially automobiles, has mastered us.

Continue buying Japanese-made cars or Korean-made cars or Mexican-made cars and maybe they will support your unemployment. What Jesus said about serving Him is true about being an American. You are either for us or you are against us. It is not the talk, it is the walk. What you have done to the least of these you have done to Him. Put your neighbor out of work—buy a foreign-made car. Francis Raleigh did that very thing while we were praying for those losing their jobs.

We Must Choose

The end is near. We have been deceived in church through our leaders. We have been deceived by our government through our leaders. We have deceived ourselves by allowing our purchase power and freedom to master us. Should we just keep on keeping on? Or should we stop living life as if it is all about me? I hope we can see that the decisions we make impact more than the lives of our spouses, children, grandchildren, great-grandchildren, and ourselves. If I purchase a foreign-made car, several Americans will lose their job over that one purchase. No matter what the name plate [Ford, Honda, Chevrolet or Kia], if it is not made in the United States, I hurt the United States.

If my pastor teaches something I know is incorrect and I keep silent, I hurt the gospel. Silence is affirmation. If my government leaders are involved in treachery, I must do what I can to right the wrong. Why am I any different than Patrick Henry, except that I am more cowardly?

God is slow to anger. He is and has been giving us every opportunity to change. He told us repeatedly over the centuries what would happen. History confirms His warnings and His carrying out His discipline. Over twenty-five thousand excavations in modern times have proven the Bible accurate each time. How much motivation does an individual need to secure eternity in a desirable place?

God gives us the right to choose in every situation. Our choices influence not only ourselves but our children, our grandchildren, and our neighbor. Who will stop the trend if it is not you? Let us, you and I, clean the wickedness from our churches. Whatever the cause or disease is, let's follow Jesus' example. Silence will bring a guilty verdict at the worst possible time.

Loving your wife, your son, your daughter, your golf clubs, your car, yourself, or anything else more or equal to God is not acceptable.

Remember Lot's wife. She cared enough for her former life to look back, and she lost everything. Whoever finds his life will lose it. Whoever loses his life for Jesus' sake will find it.

For nearly seven years, I have said no. I have asked, "Why me?" I have ignored God. I have put Him off. I have lost an entire life's savings. I have witnessed firsthand what selfish ambition will do to a man and to his effectiveness for God. And I've seen what selfish ambition does to the people around an individual driven by that kind of wickedness. All this was to bring me to an understanding of what undivided devotion means. Undivided devotion is first place. Anything less is not first place.

God spoke to His people over thirty-five hundred years ago through Moses in Deuteronomy 30:11–19, and He is still giving us the same message today, "Now what I am commanding you today is not too difficult for you or beyond your reach. It is not up in heaven, so that you have to ask, 'Who will ascend into heaven to get it and proclaim it to us so we may obey it?' Nor is it beyond the sea, so that you have to ask, 'Who will cross the sea to get it and proclaim it to us so we may obey it?' No, the Word is very near you; it is in your mouth and in your heart so you may obey it. See, I set before you today life and prosperity, death and destruction. For I command you today to love the Lord your God, to walk in His ways, and to keep His commands, decrees and laws; then you will live and increase, and the Lord your God will bless you in the land you are entering to possess. But if your heart turns away and you are not obedient, and if you are drawn away to bow down to other gods and worship them, I declare to you this day that you will certainly be destroyed. You will not live long in the land you are crossing the Jordan to enter and possess. This day I call heaven and earth as witnesses against you that I have set before you life and death, blessings and curses. Now choose life, so that you and your children may live."

Read the instruction manual. Many of us want to do it our way. Whether putting together a swing set or living life, we think we do not need the instruction manual. We assume we can do it on our own. Why would anyone decide to assume their way into God's presence for eternity?

Deception—the devil is very active and his traps are everywhere. Test everything! Be prepared through continual communication with God. You need your Bible to listen, and you need to pray. Add being silent before God, and He will give further instructions. Remember, He speaks in a soft whisper.

Today's church is described by God in Matthew 7:13–14 and Matthew 24:12. If more disciples are going to hell, falling short, than there are disciples standing firm to the end, is today's church working for God or Satan?

Let us not disappoint the creator of the universe, our sovereign Lord. Let us become His children. What an opportunity! What a responsibility!

Please, say, "Yes, Lord."

Scripture References

Leviticus 19:17b

"...Rebuke your neighbor frankly so you will not share in their guilt."

Ezekiel 3:18-21

[18] When I say to a wicked person, 'You will surely die,' and you do not warn them or speak out to dissuade them from their evil ways in order to save their life, that wicked person will die for[a] their sin, and I will hold you accountable for their blood. [19] But if you do warn the wicked person and they do not turn from their wickedness or from their evil ways, they will die for their sin; but you will have saved yourself. [20] "Again, when a righteous person turns from their righteousness and does evil, and I put a stumbling block before them, they will die. Since you did not warn them, they will die for their sin. The righteous things that person did will not be remembered, and I will hold you accountable for their blood. [21] But if you do warn the righteous person not to sin and they do not sin, they will surely live because they took warning, and you will have saved yourself."

1 John 2:21

I do not write to you because you do not know the truth, but because you do know it and because no lie comes from the truth.

Revelation 22:18-19

[18] I warn everyone who hears the words of the prophecy of this scroll: If anyone adds anything to them, God will add to that person the plagues described in this scroll. [19] And if anyone takes words away from this scroll of prophecy, God will take away from that person any share in the tree of life and in the Holy City, which are described in this scroll.

Mark 3:29

but whoever blasphemes against the Holy Spirit will never be forgiven; they are guilty of an eternal sin."

1 Corinthians 10:24

No one should seek their own good, but the good of others.

the Lord, who confirmed the message of his grace by enabling them to perform signs and wonders.

Acts 13:39

Through him everyone who believes is set free from every sin, a justification you were not able to obtain under the law of Moses.

John 1:12-13

[12] Yet to all who did receive him, to those who believed in his name, he gave the right to become children of God— [13] children born not of natural descent, nor of human decision or a husband's will, but born of God.

1 Corinthians 12:20

As it is, there are many parts, but one body.

1 Corinthians 12:12

Just as a body, though one, has many parts, but all its many parts form one body, so it is with Christ.

Micah 2:1-2

[1] Woe to those who plan iniquity, to those who plot evil on their beds! At morning's light they carry it out because it is in their power to do it. They covet fields and seize them, and houses, and take them. They defraud people of their homes, they rob them of their inheritance.

Nahum 1:3

The LORD is slow to anger but great in power; the LORD will not leave the guilty unpunished. His way is in the whirlwind and the storm, and clouds are the dust of his feet.

Micah 3:5, 7, 9

[5] This is what the LORD says: "As for the prophets who lead my people astray, they proclaim 'peace' if they have something to eat, but prepare to wage war against anyone who refuses to feed them. [7] The seers will be ashamed and the diviners disgraced. They will all cover their faces because there is no answer from God." [9] Hear this, you leaders of Jacob, you rulers of Israel, who despise justice and distort all that is right;

2 Corinthians 2:17

Unlike so many, we do not peddle the word of God for profit. On the contrary, in Christ we speak before God with sincerity, as those sent from God.

2 Thessalonians 3:7-9

[7] For you yourselves know how you ought to follow our example. We were not idle when we were with you, [8] nor did we eat anyone's food without paying for it. On the contrary, we worked night and day, laboring and toiling so that we would not be a burden to any of you. [9] We did this, not because we do not have the right to such help, but in order to offer ourselves as a model for you to imitate.

1 Corinthians 11:1

Follow my example, as I follow the example of Christ.

Philippians 4:9

Whatever you have learned or received or heard from me, or seen in me—put it into practice. And the God of peace will be with you.

1 Thessalonians 2:9

Surely you remember, brothers and sisters, our toil and hardship; we worked night and day in order not to be a burden to anyone while we preached the gospel of God to you.

Ephesians 5:6

Let no one deceive you with empty words, for because of such things God's wrath comes on those who are disobedient.

Romans 3:13

"Their throats are open graves; their tongues practice deceit." "The poison of vipers is on their lips."

Ephesians 4:14

Then we will no longer be infants, tossed back and forth by the waves, and blown here and there by every wind of teaching and by the cunning and craftiness of people in their deceitful scheming.

2 Timothy 3:13

while evildoers and impostors will go from bad to worse, deceiving and being deceived.

Jeremiah 37:9

"This is what the LORD says: Do not deceive yourselves, thinking, 'The Babylonians will surely leave us.' They will not!

1 John 2:26

I am writing these things to you about those who are trying to lead you astray.

1 John 3:7 (NAS)

Little children, make sure no one deceives you; the one who practices righteousness is righteous, just as He is righteous;

Matthew 10:37

"Anyone who loves their father or mother more than me is not worthy of me; anyone who loves their son or daughter more than me is not worthy of me.

Luke 11:23

"Whoever is not with me is against me, and whoever does not gather with me scatters.

Luke 9:62

Jesus replied, "No one who puts a hand to the plow and looks back is fit for service in the kingdom of God."

Luke 9:23-24

23 Then he said to them all: "Whoever wants to be my disciple must deny themselves and take up their cross daily and follow me. 24 For whoever wants to save their life will lose it, but whoever loses their life for me will save it.

Luke 8:21

He replied, "My mother and brothers are those who hear God's word and put it into practice."

Luke 11:52

"Woe to you experts in the law, because you have taken away the key to knowledge. You yourselves have not entered, and you have hindered those who were entering."

Luke 14:26

"If anyone comes to me and does not hate father and mother, wife and children, brothers and sisters—yes, even their own life—such a person cannot be my disciple.

1 Thessalonians 5:21

but test them all; hold on to what is good,

2 Thessalonians 2:3

Don't let anyone deceive you in any way, for that day will not come until the rebellion occurs and the man of lawlessness is revealed, the man doomed to destruction.

1 Corinthians 15:33

Do not be misled: "Bad company corrupts good character."

2 Peter 1:20-21

[20] Above all, you must understand that no prophecy of Scripture came about by the prophet's own interpretation of things. [21] For prophecy never had its origin in the human will, but prophets, though human, spoke from God as they were carried along by the Holy Spirit.

Colossians 2:8

See to it that no one takes you captive through hollow and deceptive philosophy, which depends on human tradition and the elemental spiritual forces[a] of this world rather than on Christ.

Colossians 2:3-4 (NAS)

[3] in whom are hidden all the treasures of wisdom and knowledge. [4] I say this so that no one will delude you with persuasive argument.

1 John 2:15-17

[15] Do not love the world or anything in the world. If anyone loves the world, love for the Father[a] is not in them. [16] For everything in the world—the lust of the flesh, the lust of the eyes, and the pride of life—comes not from the Father but from the world. [17] The world and its desires pass away, but whoever does the will of God lives forever.

James 4:4

You adulterous people, don't you know that friendship with the world means enmity against God? Therefore, anyone who chooses to be a friend of the world becomes an enemy of God.

James 2:17-19

[17] In the same way, faith by itself, if it is not accompanied by action, is dead. [18] But someone will say, "You have faith; I have deeds." Show me your faith without deeds, and I will show you my faith by my deeds. [19] You believe that there is one God. Good! Even the demons believe that—and shudder.

James 1:16

Don't be deceived, my dear brothers and sisters.